Little Boy Blue

A Pantomime

Paul Reakes

A SAMUEL FRENCH ACTING EDITION

SAMUEL FRENCH

FOUNDED 1830

SAMUELFRENCH.COM
SAMUELFRENCH-LONDON.CO.UK

MUSIC USE NOTE

Licensees are solely responsible for obtaining formal written permission from copyright owners to use copyrighted music in the performance of this play and are strongly cautioned to do so. If no such permission is obtained by the licensee, then the licensee must use only original music that the licensee owns and controls. Licensees are solely responsible and liable for all music clearances and shall indemnify the copyright owners of the play(s) and their licensing agent, Samuel French, against any costs, expenses, losses and liabilities arising from the use of music by licensees. Please contact the appropriate music licensing authority in your territory for the rights to any incidental music.

IMPORTANT BILLING AND CREDIT REQUIREMENTS

If you have obtained performance rights to this title, please refer to your licensing agreement for important billing and credit requirements.

CHARACTERS

The Town Crier
A Cat
Halloweena, a wicked witch
Bessie Blue, the town hall cleaner
Johnnie Blue, her son
Susie, the Mayor's daughter
Sidney Sidebottom, the Mayor of Merrydale
Fit, a footman
Mabel, a maid
Willard "Wiggles" Wigglesworth, a hot air
                    balloon man
Squawker, Halloweena's feathered familiar
The Yeti, an abominable snowman
A Woman
A Girl

Chorus of: **Townsfolk, Stallholders, Street Dancers, Wildlife, Demons, Himalayans, Zombies.**

SYNOPSIS OF SCENES

ACT I

ACT II

Time — Pantotime

MUSICAL NUMBERS

ACT I

No 1	Song and Dance	**Townsfolk**
No 2	Comedy Song and Dance	**Bessie**
No 3	Romantic Song	**Johnnie** and **Townsfolk**
No 3a	Reprise of No 3	**Susie**, **Fit** and **Mabel**
No 4	Song and Dance	**Wiggles**, **Bessie** and **Townsfolk**
No 5	Romantic Duet	**Johnnie** and **Susie**. **Wildlife** (Optional)
No 6	Song and Dance	**Townsfolk** and **Stallholders**
No 7	Dance	**Street Dancers**
No 8	Song and Dance	**All**
No 9	Dance	**Demons**
No 9a	Reprise of No 9 (Optional)	**Demons**
No 10	Song and Dance	**Cast** and the **Audience**
No 10a	Reprise of No 10	**Cast** and the **Audience**

ACT II

No 11	Song and Dance	**Himalayans**
No 12	Romantic Duet and Dance	**Johnnie** and **Susie**
No 13	Song and Dance	**Cat**, **Fit**, **Mabel** and **Himalayans**
No 13a	Reprise of No 13	**All**
No 13b	Reprise of No 9 (Optional)	**Demons**
No 14	Comedy "Evil" Song and Dance	**Halloweena** and **Squawker**
No 15	Song and Dance	**Zombies**
No 16	Song and Dance	**All**
No 17	Community Song	**Fit**, **Mabel** and the **Audience**
No 18	Finale Song or Reprise	**All**

CHARACTERS AND COSTUMES

The Town Crier must obviously have a loud, clear voice. He wears the full regalia and has a handbell and scroll.

A Cat (Female/Child's part) This is indeed a miraculous cat. She can understand human speech, communicate with people and even instigate dance routines! Despite these amazing attributes, she still has all the mannerisms and characteristics of an ordinary moggy. Ear and whisker cleaning, with the occasional bout of scratching, would not be out of place. Agility is needed, and above all, the ability to make the animal lovable to the audience. A good cat costume with mask or facial make-up. A cat collar with what appears to be diamond studs.

Halloweena (Baddie) is, as she keeps telling us, the wickedest witch in the world! She is a very unpleasant individual who revels in her own villainy. She never misses an opportunity of stirring the audience into a frenzy of boos and hisses. This is strong character part and must be able to give as good as she gets. She should not be portrayed as the "old crone" variety of witch. She can even be attractive in a macabre way. A small amount of singing and dancing is required. With her bizarrely spectacular costumes, make-up and headdresses, she is the personification of fashionable evilness.

Bessie Blue (Dame) is the town hall cleaner. She is a buxom, blousy "lady" who changes her mood at the drop of a hat. Motherly and mirthful one minute, sarcastic and cynical the next. She can also be comically seductive and sexy. Whatever her mood, you can't help liking her. She is always on friendly and confidential terms with the audience and never misses a opportunity of involving them. Singing and dancing ability is an advantage, but good comic timing is essential. It goes without saying that all her costumes, hair-dos and make-up are ludicrous and funny. A gaudy overall and turban for her cleaning job and a fancy outfit for the fete in Act I Scene 3. She will need a quick change costume that displays her recently acquired wealth in Act II Scene 4. An outrageous wedding dress for the Finale.

Johnnie Blue (Principal Boy) and **Susie** (Principal Girl) Johnnie is Bessie's son. A handsome, likeable young man. Susie is the Mayor's daughter. A pretty, likeable young woman. Singing and dancing ability is needed for both these roles, as well as good camaraderie with the audience. They are deeply in love with each other. But as Johnnie is from a poor family, the Mayor has forbidden them to see each other.

And this is not their only problem. After befriending Halloweena's cat, the witch takes her revenge by putting a curse on them — turning them completely blue! Skin, hair, clothes! The lot! I'm sure your excellent costume and make-up departments will have their own ideas on how to achieve this bit of magic! Obviously it means that blue duplicates of their costumes are required. These should be made so that only the minimum of flesh requires blue make-up. (Please make sure that you use a tried and tested body paint) Legs should be concealed by tights or leggings. In both cases wigs can be used, but for Johnnie, I suggest that his hair be completely hidden under a cap or hat. Magnificent wedding costumes for the Finale.

Sidney Sidebottom is the Mayor of Merrydale. He is full of self-importance and a snob. The personification of parochial pomposity. This makes him a figure of fun and ridicule. Especially with Bessie, who enjoys reminding him of his lowly origins. He refers to her and her family as riff-raff. However, when they become rich he soon changes his tune and wants to make Bessie his wife! Ideally, he should be a short man and corpulent. Singing and dancing ability is not required. He wears his mayoral chain all the time. He probably sleeps in it! For the opening of the fête, he wears his official robe and hat. This is worn for the Finale.

Fit and **Mabel** (Comedy Duo) Although not overburdened with brains, they are a very likeable couple. They can be ridiculously "lovey-dovey" with each other at times. Mostly they are just plain goofy! Singing and dancing ability is an advantage, but good rapport and camaraderie with the audience is essential. They are involved in plenty of comic business and audience participation. Ideally, Fit should be tall and skinny, while Mabel is petite and buxom. He wears footman's livery that is too small, and she wears a maid's uniform that is too ... Well, short would be the understatement of the year! For the Finale, Mabel adds a wedding veil and carries a bouquet. Fit adds a fancy hat and huge button hole.

Willard "Wiggles" Wigglesworth is the owner of a hot air balloon. He is an urbane gentleman of the old school. Rather vague and detached, but very pleasant and courteous. The poor man becomes Bessie's love interest without being aware of it! A small amount of singing and dancing is required. He joins Bessie in plenty of comic business and audience participation. He wears overalls, an old-fashioned leather flying helmet, goggles, a scarf and boots. Wedding outfit for the Finale.

Squawker (Male or Female part) is a giant bird! It is the witch's feathered familiar. It has perfect understanding of human speech and can talk, albeit with an awful, rasping croak. It is not essential to be able to fly for this role, but appearing to do so is necessary! This mainly applies to the scene in which it attacks the hot air balloon. Mostly it just hops about, flapping its wings and squawking. Even amongst the audience! A small amount of singing and dancing is required. Comically repulsive to look at, this oversized oddity should be a costume designer's dream — or nightmare!

The Yeti is the abominable snowman. It is huge, hideous and hairy. It is completely white, has claws and fangs and a tremendous roar. Unless you have a real Yeti in captivity, this part will have to be played by a tall male actor in a shaggy white costume! No singing or dancing is required. Just the ability to behave fiercely until it meets the Cat and becomes friendly with everyone. It only appears in Act II. A fancy hat and bow tie for the Finale.

A Woman and **A Girl** are the Yeti and the Cat after the witch's curse has been lifted. The woman is a white witch who only uses her magic for good. The Girl is her daughter and apprentice. They had been transformed by Halloweena. Graceful movement and pleasant speaking voices are necessary for these two roles. Their ethereal appearance and diaphanous costumes leave us in no doubt that they are from another dimension. The Girl wears a duplicate of the cat's diamond studded collar. They only appear in Act II.

The **Chorus**, **Dancers** and **Children** appear as **Townsfolk**, **Stallholders**, **Wildlife**, **Street Dancers**, **Demons**, **Himalayan Natives** and **Zombies**. All participate in the action and musical numbers. The Townsfolk should be a mixture of gentry and peasantry and costumed accordingly. The Stallholders are clothed in picturesque homespun, and the Street Dancers are colourful and gypsy-like. The Wildlife (optional) are fluffy rabbits and squirrels, etc. The little Demons are in red with facial make-up or devil masks. The Himalayan Natives wear fur-trimmed outfits with hoods, mittens and snow boots. The Zombies are dressed in a variety of rotting rags, with matted hair and decomposed complexions.

PRODUCTION NOTES

The pantomime offers opportunities for elaborate staging, but can be produced quite simply if funds and facilities are limited.

There are four full sets:
> Merrydale Town Square
> The Grand Fête
> Somewhere in the Himalayas
> Swamp on the Witch's Island

There is one half set:
> Up In The Air

These scenes are interlinked by tabs, or two front cloths:
> Lovers' Lane
> The Witch's Lair

There can be a special Finale setting, or the Town Square set can be used with added decorations.

STAGING

Merrydale Town Square is surrounded by picturesque shops and buildings. On one side, steps lead to the pillared entrance of the town hall. In the distance is a field with tents and stalls ready for the forthcoming fête. There is also a hot air balloon. (See Distant Balloon notes) The Grand Fête shows a field with colourful tents and stalls. There are flags and bunting. At the back is a small rostrum. Among other signs, there is one reading BALLOON RIDES! THIS WAY. A view of sky and countryside in the distance. Somewhere in the Himalayas is a mountain pass, edged by snow-covered rocks and boulders. At the back is a large boulder which conceals the Yeti. In the distance there are huge snow-capped mountains and glaciers. The scene has a bleak, but clean and sparkling beauty. Swamp on the Witch's Island is a complete contrast. Gnarled and twisted trees overhang the steamy swamp. Dense undergrowth and tangled creepers abound. In the distance can be seen the rest of the volcanic island under a strange, multi-coloured sky. Lovers' Lane is a front cloth representing a picturesque country lane. The Witch's Lair is another front cloth showing the interior of a spooky cave with bizarre wall paintings. These cloths are used to interlink the full set scenes. If this is not practical, tabs can be used.

Up In The Air (Act I Scene 5)
In this scene our intrepid adventurers are seen travelling by hot air balloon in search of the evil witch. The following are only suggestions of how to create this effect. I am sure individual directors and set designers will have their own excellent ideas. This is a half set. The backcloth shows blue sky with fluffy white clouds. The side wings represent sky and clouds. A ground row of clouds extends across the stage from wing to wing. In the centre, behind the ground row, is the basket of the balloon. This can be made from actual basketwork or a light construction painted to represent a basket. Whatever is used, it needs to be bottomless. Ropes are attached to each corner of the basket. The other ends of these ropes are secured up in the flies. This will give the impression that they are attached to the actual balloon which is out of sight. The basket should be suspended above the stage by about eight inches. (The gap is covered by the cloud ground row) This will allow it to swing freely from side to side. Standing inside the basket, the cast, by holding the edges or the ropes, can simulate its movements in the air. This will be particularly effective during the giant bird's attack and the storm sequence. Another method would be to have the basket on castors. The ropes can be kept rigid by winding stiff wire around them. If facilities make any of the above impractical, the basket can be stationary with the ropes wired and disappearing into the flies.

Distant Balloon (Act I, Scenes 1 and 3. Act II, Scenes 1 and 3)

In these scenes the hot air balloon is viewed in the distance. Act I Scene 1 is the easy one. As it is seen to be stationary in a field it can be painted on the backcloth. In the other scenes it's on the move! This is always at the back of the stage, close to the backcloth. It appears to float into view from one side, drift across the sky, and float out on the other side. In Act II Scene 1 it is seen to be tossed about in a mighty storm. The simplest method of "flight" is by running a model or painted cut-out on lines or wires. Once again, this is only a suggestion. I'm sure your director or set designer will achieve another minor miracle.

Lighting

Bright general lighting for the Town Square, Grand Fête and Lovers' Lane scenes. Romantic lighting changes are required for all the love songs and duets. The lighting for the Witch's Lair should be dark and spooky. Sinister lighting change for Halloweena's entrances. Flashes of lightning are frequently used, particularly in the spectacular storm sequence at the end of Act I. The scene in the Himalayas requires a falling snow effect at the opening. This is followed by a short storm sequence, and then the effect of sunlight on snow for the rest of the scene. The Swamp should be a complete contrast. A reddish glow lights the scene, illuminating the twisted trees and tangled creepers. This will help to create a hot and steamy atmosphere. Also, there are dark shadows in which anything might be lurking! A thoroughly unpleasant place altogether. It's even more creepy when the repulsive zombies come looking for their dinner! Several complete black-outs are required as characters "magically" appear and disappear. Further use of follow spots for entrances, musical numbers and audience participation, etc. is left to the discretion of the individual director.

Effects

All the usual elements are required for a tale of magic and adventure. Blinding flashes and black-outs as characters appear and disappear. Weird and unearthly sounds to accompany the Witch in her evil doings and incantations. A tempestuous storm scene with thunder and lightning, howling winds and lashing rain. A blizzard of snow and ice. A steamy swamp with swirling, but well controlled, ground mist. An off stage microphone is required so that the Witch's voice and evil laughter can be heard coming out of the air. Any other effects to enhance the production may be added at the director's discretion.

The time is Pantotime. This means that the style of settings and costumes can be a fantastical mixture of all periods. Enjoy!

Paul Reakes

Other works by Paul Reakes
published by Samuel French Ltd

Pantomimes

Babes in the Wood
Bluebeard
Cinderella
Dick Turpin
Goody Two Shoes
King Arthur
King Humpty Dumpty
Little Bo Peep
Little Jack Horner
Little Miss Muffet
Little Red Riding Hood
Little Tommy Tucker
Old King Cole
Old Mother Hubbard
Robinson Crusoe and the Pirates
Santa in Space
Sinbad the Sailor
Tom Thumb

Plays

Bang, You're Dead!
Mantrap

ACT I

SCENE 1

Merrydale Town Square

Full set. The side wings represent picturesque shops and buildings. On L are steps leading to the pillared entrance of the Town Hall. The backcloth shows a distant field with tents, stalls and a hot air balloon. (See Production Notes) Entrances R and L and at the back

When the CURTAIN *rises, the Chorus, as Townsfolk, are discovered going about their business. This develops into a lively song and dance*

Song 1

After the number, a bell is heard ringing

The Town Crier, in full regalia, enters from R. He moves to C, finishes ringing his bell and reads from a scroll

Town Crier (*in a loud clear voice*) *Oyez! Oyez! Oyez!* Today, at two of the clock, the grand fête of Merrydale will be opened by His Worship the Mayor! *Oyez! Oyez! Oyez!*

Ringing his bell, the Town Crier exits L

The Townsfolk gather and show their excitement

1st Townsperson I can't wait for the fête to open!
2nd Townsperson Neither can I. I'm dying to have a ride in that hot air balloon!
Others Oh, yes! Same here! (*Etc.*)

They all turn upstage to look at the balloon in the distance

A large female Cat bounds on from R. She pauses at C to clean her ears and whiskers

She then catches sight of the audience, and with a meowed greeting, waves her paw at them. The Townsfolk turn and see the Cat. The Children move down to stroke and pet the animal

Halloweena (*off* R, *yelling angrily*) Cat?! Where are you?! Come to me at once! CAAAAT!!!

Terrified, the Cat runs out L

The lighting becomes dark and sinister. All react

Halloweena sweeps on from R. *She is weirdly dressed and terrifying in appearance*

(*Still calling*) Cat! Where are you? Just wait till I get my hands on you! I'll —— (*She sees the Children*) Oh! What have we got here? (*She approaches them and snarls*) Grr! It's children! Nasty, smelly children! (*Snarling at them*) Tell me, you little brats, have you seen my cat?
Children No!
Halloweena (*to Townsfolk*) Have you?
Townsfolk No!
Halloweena Oh, yes, you have!
Children ⎫
          ⎬ (*together*) Oh, no, we haven't!
Townsfolk ⎭
Halloweena Oh, yes, you have!

The Children and Townsfolk encourage the audience to join them. This continues ad-lib

Halloweena (*snarling at the audience*) Who invited *you* to join in anyway? Who are you? *What* are you? Are you the annual outing of the ugliest uglies? (*She gives an evil cackle*) Hee! Hee! Hee! Oh, no! I can see more nasty, smelly, revolting children! Grr! I hate children! You're horrible little maggots! What are you?

By-play with the audience

Be warned! I am Halloweena! The wickedest witch in the world! Any more insults and I will be forced to use my magic powers on you! Oh, yes, I will!

Routine with the audience

Grr! Enough of this! (*Sweeping to exit* L) I'm going now! But don't think you've seen the last of Halloweena! The wickedest witch in the world! Ha! Ha! Ha!

Laughing her evil laugh, she sweeps out L, *amid boos and hisses*

The lighting returns to normal

Loud, atrocious singing is heard coming from inside the Town Hall

The rear end of Bessie Blue appears in the entrance. She is on her knees and is scrubbing the floor using a brush and pail. Singing at the top of her voice, she makes her way down the steps. She continues scrubbing across the stage and ends up polishing the shoes of one of the Townsfolk

Bessie (*peering at the shoes*) Eh?! (*She looks up and sees the crowd*) Oh! (*She stands up; brightly*) Mornin' all!
Townsfolk Morning, Bessie!
Bessie (*to the owner of the shoes*) That'll be two pounds, please. For an extra fifty pence I'll polish yer teeth as well. (*Holding out her hand*) Come on, whip 'em out and 'and 'em over!

Bessie laughs, but the other is stone-faced

All the Townsfolk and Children exit in various directions

(*To the audience, absently*) No sense of humour! Must be from [local place]! (*Suddenly aware of the audience, she reacts*) *Crikey!!* It's a plot of leeple! (*Coming forward and greeting the audience*) Hello!

There are a few replies

Oh, come on! There's no need to be shy. (*Loudly*) *Hello!*

They call back

That's better. Well, it's nice to see all of you. (*To a male*) Not that I can see all of you, young man, but I'm sure it's very nice! My name's Bessie. Bessie Blue. I'm the cleaner at the town hall. It's my job to keep the dust at bay and give all the knobs a good rub. My mother had the job before me, an' her mother had it before her. So you could say I come from a long line of old scrubbers! You were waitin' for that one, weren't yah? And here's something else you've all been waiting for. Another chance to hear me sing. Oh, yes! And if you don't clap I'll sing it six more times! (*She throws or kicks the brush and bucket into the town hall.* To *Conductor/Pianist*) Take it away, Sir Andrew!

Song 2

A comedy song and dance for Bessie

(*After the song*) I'm a widow too, by the way. (*She sighs*) Ahh! (*She encourages the audience to sigh*) No, I've been a widow for much longer than that. I'm not completely on me own though. I've got a lovely son. And he's so good to his old mum. His name's Johnnie. Johnnie Blue. He's always been called Little Boy Blue. I can't think why. He's not so little anymore. In fact ... (*She looks to off* R) Oh! Here he comes now. You can see for yourselves.

Handsome young Johnnie Blue enters from R. *He is distracted and keeps looking towards the town hall*

(*Going to him*) Hello, Johnnie!

No response

Johnnie?
Johnnie (*not listening and looking towards the town hall*) Huh?
Bessie I'll give you "*huh*"! I said hello.
Johnnie (*as before*) Huh?
Bessie (*pulling his head round to face her*) Look at me when I'm talkin' to yah!
Johnnie Oh! Hello, Mum.
Bessie That's better.

She releases him and he looks at the town hall again

There's some nice people 'ere I'd like you to meet.
Johnnie Huh?
Bessie (*to the audience*) Tch! Kids! Who'd 'ave 'em! (*To Johnnie*) Now, look 'ere ...

Johnnie walks straight past her and goes to the foot of the town hall steps. He looks up at the entrance, longingly

Johnnie Blue! Don't be so flippin' rude! (*She marches over to Johnnie and turns his head as before*)
Johnnie Hello, Mum. Are you here again?
Bessie Course I am! Stop showin' me up in front of all these people.
Johnnie What people?
Bessie (*turning his face to the audience*) Them people!
Johnnie Oh! (*To the audience*) Hello!
Audience Hello!

Bessie releases him and he goes straight back to gazing at the town hall entrance

Bessie Where will they think you was brung up? Didn't they teach you any manners at [local school/college]? I said, didn't they —— (*She turns and sees him gazing at the entrance*) Johnnie!
Johnnie (*looking at her*) Hello, Mum. Is there something wrong?
Bessie I'll say there is! All you seem interested in is the town hall. What's so fascinatin' about that old dump? You've seen it hundreds of times before.
Johnnie I'm waiting for someone to come out. Someone special. (*All dreamy*) The girl I love! (*With a big sigh*) Susie!
Bessie And who's (*copying the sigh*) Susie?
Johnnie Susie Sidebottom.
Bessie (*aghast*) Susie Sidebottom! You don't mean Mayor Sidebottom's daughter?!
Johnnie Yes. (*Rapturously*) I love her with all my heart! (*He gives an even bigger sigh*)
Bessie (*to audience*) Crikey! He's got it worse than [TV soap character]!
Johnnie And Susie reciprocates.
Bessie (*making a wry face*) Does she? I think you can get a cream for that.
Johnnie I mean she feels the same way about me. We want to be married.
Bessie (*scoffing*) And I wanna be [current beauty]! Does old Sidebottom know about this?
Johnnie Well ... he knows we've been seeing each other and he's not very happy about it.
Bessie Why not?
Johnnie Well, he is the Mayor. And I'm only a poor boy from a poor family. (*He sadly hangs his head*)
Bessie (*sighing*) Ahhh! (*She encourages the audience to join in. Finally, she puts her arm around Johnnie*) We may be poor, Johnnie, but we're respectable. Our family's got nothing to be ashamed of. Better not mention yer Uncle Cynthia.
Johnnie Uncle Cynthia?

Bessie I said not to mention him. Listen to me, son. If you really love
Susie Sidebottom you go after her. Never mind what her father thinks.
Johnnie (*brightening*) You're right, Mum. Like that old saying — love
levels all ranks!
Bessie (*inspired*) Yeah! And a watched pot never lays all its eggs in
one basket! (*She strides to the exit* R, *and then turns to give Johnnie a
"thumbs up"*) Go for it, my son!
Johnnie Thanks, Mum!
Bessie (*to the audience*) Isn't he a lovely lad? Smashin' legs too. They
run in our family, y'know! Like big noses! Bye! See you later!

Bessie gives the audience a wave and exits

Johnnie turns to look at the hall entrance

The Townsfolk drift on from various directions

Eventually, Johnnie turns to face front

Johnnie (*with a sigh*) Where on earth can Susie be? She told me to meet
her here this morning. I hope her father hasn't stopped her coming out.
Oh, I can't wait to see her again. I love her so much, you see.

Song 3

A romantic song and dance for Johnnie and the Townsfolk

After the number, Johnnie moves to the hall and sits on the steps

The Townsfolk drift out in various directions

*After a while, Johnnie gets despondently to his feet and addresses the
audience*

I don't think Susie's coming out, do you? What shall I do? I can't
hang about here. Her father may come along and cause a fuss. I know!
I'll go to our secret meeting place. Lovers' Lane. Will you do me a
favour, folks? If you see Susie will you tell her I'm waiting for her in
Lover's Lane? You will? That's great! Thanks!

With a wave, he exits R

*After a slight pause, pretty young Susie Sidebottom appears in the hall
entrance. She looks about cautiously*

Susie (*calling, softly*) Johnnie? Are you there? ... Johnnie? (*She comes down the steps and searches the deserted square*) Johnnie? ... Johnnie? ... Oh, no! ... He's not here! I wonder ... (*She spots the audience*) Oh! (*She greets them with a very pleasant smile*) Hello ... Hello. How d'you do. I'm Susie Sidebottom. The Mayor's daughter. Oh! You've heard of me? Well, I'm not surprised with a name like Sidebottom. But *how* have you heard of me?

"From Johnnie!" etc.

From Johnnie! Then you've seen him? Do you know where he is now?

"Lovers' Lane" etc.

Lovers' Lane! Is he waiting there for me? Oh, good! I'll go there straight away. Thank you very much.

Susie runs to the exit R

Suddenly, the corpulent figure of the Sidney Sidebottom, the Mayor, appears in the town hall entrance. He is wearing his mayoral chain

Mayor (*calling to her, loudly*) Susie!
Susie (*stopping in her tracks and turning*) Oh! Hello, Daddy.
Mayor (*coming down the steps*) Where are you going to in such a hurry?
Susie Nowhere.
Mayor It didn't look like it. I hope you're not running after that good-for-nothing, Little Boy Blue.
Susie I do wish you wouldn't call him that.
Mayor Why not? That's what he's called, isn't he? (*Contemptuously*) *Little Boy Blue!* Huh! Stupid name for a fully-grown lad, if you ask me.
Susie It's just a nickname from when he was a little boy. Besides, I wasn't referring to that. I wish you wouldn't call him a good-for-nothing.
Mayor Well, that's what he is. And a *penniless* good-for-nothing to boot. His whole family's as poor as church mice. Bessie Blue, that mother of his, works for us as a cleaner. And I know how poor *she* is because I pay her wages. (*Pompously*) As Mayor of this town I have a reputation to maintain. I can't have my only daughter associating with a family of riff-raff.
Susie (*angrily*) Oh, Daddy! How can you say that? You were born in the same street as Bessie Blue! You went to school with her!

Mayor Yes, I did. But *I* made something of myself. I dragged myself out of the sleazy slums and ascended to the sparkling heights of local government and commerce. I rose to become (*striking a pompous pose*) His Worship, the Mayor of Merrydale!

Susie (*to the audience*) That's what happens if you read/watch too many Catherine Cooksons.

Mayor (*to Susie*) Now, get inside where I can keep an eye on you.

Susie (*defiantly*) I won't! I'm going to see Johnnie whether you like it or not.

She marches towards the exit R

Mayor (*grabbing her by the arm*) Oh, no, you don't! (*Yelling towards the hall*) Oi! You two! Fit and Mabel! Get out here at once!

Fit, the Footman, and Mabel, the maid, appear in the town hall entrance. They come down the steps and stand gaping at the struggling couple

(*Seeing them and yelling*) Don't just stand there, you couple of clowns! Grab hold! ... GRAB HOLD!!

Comic business as Fit and Mabel rush across and grab hold of the Mayor

(*Yelling at them*) Not *me!* ... Not *me*, you dozy dunderheads! Miss Susie! Grab Miss Susie!

Fit and Mabel let go of him and take hold of Susie. She doesn't struggle. The Mayor sorts himself out

I haven't got time for this nonsense. I've got a hundred and one things to do before I open the fête this afternoon. Fit and Mabel!

Duo Yes, Your Worship?

Mayor I've got a special job for you.

Duo Yes, Your Worship!

Mayor I want you to keep a close watch on Miss Susie. Don't take your eyes off her.

Duo Yes, Your Worship! No, Your Worship!

Susie (*protesting*) Father!

Mayor Quiet! (*To Duo*) And above all, don't let her have anything to do with Little Boy Blue. (*Sternly*) Is that clear?

Duo Yes, Your Worship!

Susie Father, you can't do this!

Mayor I *can* and I *have*. (*He goes to the town hall entrance and turns*) And if I find out you've let them see each other, you can both look for another job! We won't have any of that Downton Abbey nonsense here!

The Mayor exits into the hall

Mabel Oh, Miss Susie! What have you been up to?
Fit More to the point, what have you and Little Boy Blue been up to?

Fit and Mabel giggle

Susie I'll tell you if you let me go.
Fit We can't do that, Miss Susie. You heard what the old ... er ... you heard what your father said. (*He holds on to her tightly*) I'm not to take my eyes of you.
Susie That doesn't include your hands.
Mabel She's right! (*She disentangles Fit from Susie and pulls him away from her*) You're spoken for! Don't forget that!
Fit How could I? (*Going all soppy*) My little sugar plum!
Mabel (*equally soppy*) My little lambkins!

Comic business as they canoodle together. While this is happening, Susie creeps away towards the exit R

(*Spotting Susie and yelling*) Miss Susie!

The pair of them run across and bring Susie back

Fit You mustn't do that, Miss Susie.
Mabel You'll get us the sack.
Susie But I have to go and see Johnnie. He's waiting for me in Lovers' Lane. We can't bear to be apart. We love each other so much. You know what it's like to be in love, don't you?
Duo (*all soppy again*) Oooh, yes!
Susie It's the most wonderful feeling in the world.
Duo Oooh, yes!

Reprise of Song 3

The lighting becomes romantic. As Susie sings, Fit and Mabel are greatly affected and comically overcome with emotion. Eventually, they take over the singing

During this, Susie sneaks away and exits R

Fit and Mabel finish singing and dance together. Suddenly, they realize Susie has gone and let out a yell. This stops the music and the lighting snaps back to normal. In a panic, they run to the exit R

At that moment Bessie enters R

Needless to say there is a collision! Bessie is knocked to the ground. Fit and Mabel make for the exit

Bessie (*on her back, yelling*) Oi! Come back! Don't leave me down 'ere! 'Elp me up!

Comic business and ad-lib as Fit and Mabel haul Bessie to her feet

(*Adjusting her clothing*) Look what you've done to my twin-set! What's all the panic about? Are [local reference] having a sale?

Suddenly, a loud crash is heard in the town hall. This is followed by yells of agony and rage

The Townsfolk rush on from all directions to see what the noise is about

The Mayor appears in the hall entrance. He is dishevelled and has a bucket stuck on one foot

Bessie and the Crowd find this very amusing

Fit and Mabel give a yell and run out R

Fuming with rage, the Mayor hobbles down the steps

'Ullo, Your Washup! Looks like you've put yer foot in it! Is this the latest thing from [fashion designer]? I don't think it'll catch on.
Mayor (*fuming*) This is your fault, Bessie Blue! Leaving your mops and buckets lying about all over the place! I could have had a very nasty accident.
Bessie Lookin' at yer face, I thought you had!
Mayor Stop being asinine!
Bessie Ooh! Wash yer mouth out! (*Lifting his chain*) What happens if I pull this? Do you flush?
Mayor Leave that alone! Get this thing off me!

Comic business as Bessie attempts to get the bucket off the Mayor's foot.
After many contortions, she manages to remove it and throws it into the
town hall

Bessie (*to Mayor*) Now you're — *beyond the pail!* Ta Tra! (*To the*
audience) Well, what d'you expect — [topical comedian]?!
Mayor And another thing. I want you to stop your son from seeing my
daughter.
Bessie (*bridling*) Oh! And why is that, pray?
Mayor Surely it's obvious. Even to someone of your perspicacity.
Bessie (*to the audience*) If I knew what that meant I'd be livid!
Mayor (*pompously*) As Mayor I am very prominent in this area. (*He*
puffs out his chest)
Bessie (*glancing at his rear*) In *all* areas, if you ask me!
Mayor I have a position to uphold.
Bessie So do I. Scrum half for [local Rugby team]!
Mayor I cannot have my daughter hob-nobbing with the likes of your
son. And ——
Bessie 'Ere! Hold yer hob and yer knob a minute! Are you insineratin'
our family's rubbish?
Mayor In a word — yes!
Bessie (*getting her dander up*) Ooh! Well, *I've* got a word for *you!*
Snob! That's what *you* are, Sidney Sidebottom! *A snob!* You're no
better than me! We were both dragged up in the same gutter! Your
family were so poor yer mum had to put *two* babies in *one* nappy. It
was the only way she could make ends meet! (*She advances on him*)

The Mayor backs away

So! Don't you get all high and mighty with me, Sidney Sidebottom!
My family's just as good as yours! And don't you forget it!

The Mayor backs into the town hall steps and falls over. He is soon on
his feet and makes a hasty exit into the town hall

Bessie and the Townsfolk laugh

The Cat bounds on from L. *She pauses at* C *to catch her breath*

Halloweena (*off* L, *yelling angrily*) Cat! Come back here! CAAAAT!!!

The Cat runs out R

Halloweena storms on from L. *As she crosses, she angrily pushes Bessie out of her way and exits* R

Bessie (*to the audience*) Charmin'! (*To someone, coming forward*) Is she a friend of yours, dear? No? I only asked because it looks like you both go to the same hairdressers!

Unseen by Bessie, Willard "Wiggles" Wigglesworth enters at the back. A pleasant, urbane gentleman of the old school, he wears overalls, an old-fashioned leather flying helmet, goggles, boots and a scarf

The Townsfolk react as he makes his way down to beside the unsuspecting Bessie. Oblivious, she chats away to various members of the audience. Some will probably be trying to draw her attention to the strange figure beside her. Finally, she sees Wiggles and leaps back with a frightened yell

Ahhgh!! It's a giant frog!
Wiggles (*genially*) Good-morning.
Bessie A giant *talkin'* frog!
Wiggles (*pushing the goggles on to his forehead*) I'm most awfully sorry if I gave you a bit of a turn. The name's Wigglesworth. Willard Wigglesworth. Wiggles to you.
Bessie (*affronted*) And the same to *you* with knobs on!
Wiggles No, no. Wiggles is my nickname. Short for Wigglesworth.
Bessie I'm Bessie, short for ... er ... my age! What are you doing in Merrydale, Giggles ... er ... Waggles ... er ... Wiggles?
Wiggles We're here for the fête this afternoon. Me and the old girl.
Bessie Your wife?
Wiggles (*laughing*) Ha! Ha! Lord, no! I'm a bachelor.
Bessie (*very interested*) Are yah? (*Holding out her hand, very seductively*) Hello. Charmed ever so muchly I'm sure!
Wiggles (*shaking her hand*) Yes ... I was talking about my hot air balloon! (*He turns and proudly points to the distant balloon*) There she is! My pride and joy! Awfully grand, isn't she? I've been hired to give rides at the fête.
Bessie Well, you won't get *me* up in of them things! I like to keep *my* feet on good old terracotta.
Wiggles You don't know what you're missing! There's nothing like it. Floating above the clouds with the wind in your hair.
Bessie And yer stomach in yer mouth!
Wiggles I'm sure you'd like it if you gave it a try.
Bessie (*nudging him*) Cheeky! I bet you say that to all the girls!

Song 4

A song for Wiggles involving Bessie and the Townsfolk

After the number and applause, there is a loud crash and a yell in the town hall

> *The Mayor staggers into view. This time he has a bucket stuck on his head!*

Quick black-out

Music to cover the scene change, and then the Lights come up on —

SCENE 2

Lover's Lane

Tabs, or a front cloth showing a picturesque country lane. Entrances DR *and* DL

> *The Cat bounds on from* DL. *She pauses at* C *to meow and wave to the audience*

Halloweena (*off* DL, *yelling*) Cat! Where are you?! CAAAAT!!

The Cat runs out DR

The lighting becomes dark and sinister

> *Halloweena sweeps on from* DL. *She is met with a barrage of abuse from the audience*

> (*Snarling at them*) So! You're still here, are you? I thought I could smell something nasty! You miserable mob of mouldy misfits! Grr!! Why don't you go and hire yourselves out as dartboards! (*She gives her evil laugh*) Hee! Hee! Hee! Have you seen that wretched cat of mine?
Audience No!
Halloweena Oh, yes, you have!
Audience Oh, no, we haven't!

This continues ad-lib

Halloweena Well, I don't care if you have or you haven't! I'll soon find that mutinous moggy! And when I do, it'll wish it had never been born! And the same applies to you if I have any more of your cheek! Grrr!!

Snarling at the audience, Halloweena exits DR

The lighting returns to normal

Johnnie enters from DL. *He looks about and then spots the audience*

Johnnie (*coming forward and greeting the audience*) Hello, folks! Hi, kids! Did you see Susie?
Audience Yes.
Johnnie She's nice, isn't she?
Audience Yes.
Johnnie And did you tell her that I'd be waiting for her here in Lovers' Lane?
Audience Yes.
Johnnie Thanks a lot. (*He looks about*) Well, where is she? I'll give her a call. (*Calling*) Susie! ... *Susie!* (*He looks about*) Perhaps she didn't hear. Will you help me call Susie, kids?
Audience Yes!
Johnnie Great! After three. One, two, three!

He and the audience call

Susie! (*He looks about*) No. Let's try again. Louder this time. One, two, three!

They call again

Susie!

Unseen by Johnnie, Susie enters from DL. *She creeps up behind him*

The audience will be calling out, but Johnnie takes no notice and looks from side to side

No, still nothing. She *must* have heard that. I bet they could hear it in [far off local place]! I wonder what's happened to her?

Playfully, Susie puts her hands over Johnnie's eyes

Ahh! Who's that?

Susie (*in a disguised voice*) Guess who?

Johnnie knows who it is, but plays along

Johnnie Is it [name of current personality]?
Susie No. Try again.
Johnnie Oh, I give up!
Susie *It's me!*

She whips away her hands. They joyously fall into each other's arms

Johnnie I knew it was you all along.
Susie How?
Johnnie Because of your great big hairy hands!
Susie (*playfully slapping him*) You! (*Indicating the audience*) Have you thanked our friends for helping us?
Johnnie Yes.
Susie They're really very nice, aren't they?
Johnnie Yes. Unlike someone I could mention.
Susie My father?
Johnnie Who else?
Susie You haven't heard the latest. He's got Fit and Mabel guarding me. They're to make sure you and I never see each other. (*Getting tearful*) It's — it's not fair.
Johnnie (*comforting her*) Don't get upset, Susie. No matter what your father says or does, we still love each other. And we always will.

Song 5

A romantic duet with romantic lighting

NOTE: If desired, a few small children, as Wildlife, can enter and dance around the young lovers

After the number, the lighting returns to normal

If used, the Wildlife exit

Susie I suppose we'd better be getting back.
Johnnie Yes. We don't want to get Fit and Mabel into trouble.

Hand in hand, they make for the DL exit

The Cat runs on from DR. *She pulls up short at the sight of Johnnie and Susie*

Susie (*seeing the Cat*) Oh, Johnnie, look!
Johnnie Oh! Hello, puss.

They move towards the Cat. She timidly backs away from them

There's no need to be afraid. We're not going to hurt you. (*He kneels and holds out his hand*) Come on, puss ... come on.

Cautiously, the Cat moves over. Very soon she's allowing Johnnie and Susie to stroke and pet her

Cat Meow! Meow!
Susie You're a lovely pussy cat, aren't you?
Cat (*nodding*) Meow! Meow!
Johnnie (*standing up*) And intelligent too. (*To the audience*) Must have been on *Purr*fection!
Susie I wonder who it belongs to?
Halloweena (*off* DR, *yelling*) CAAAAT!!

Terrified, the Cat cowers against Johnnie and Susie. The lighting becomes dark and sinister

Halloweena sweeps on from DR

(*Seeing the Cat*) Ah! There you are, you wretched animal! I'll teach you to run away from me! Come here at once, you confounded creature! (*With evil relish*) Come here!
Johnnie I don't think she wants to. Do you, puss?
Cat (*shaking its head*) Meow! Meow!
Halloweena What's this got to do with *you* anyway? That cat belongs to *me* and I'll treat it any way I choose!
Susie Not while we're here, you won't.
Halloweena Bah! Enough of this! Give me that cat!

Halloweena crosses to make a grab for Cat. Johnnie gives her a hefty push and she falls over. The audience greatly enjoy this. Cat, Johnnie and Susie give each other high fives. Halloweena staggers to her feet

(*To Johnnie, seething with rage*) Grr! You will regret doing that, you meddlesome moron! (*To Cat*) And so will *you*! Come here, so that I can pull out all your whiskers! (*With evil relish*) One at a time!

Cat (*scared*) Meow!
Susie (*confronting Halloweena*) You ought to be ashamed of yourself. Wanting to treat a poor defenceless animal like that. Go away before I report you.
Johnnie I think we should report her anyway. For being so gross! (*To the audience*) Don't you, folks?
Audience Yes!
Halloweena (*to the audience*) Oh, crawl back under your stones! (*To Johnnie and Susie*) Do you know who I am?
Susie As if we cared!
Halloweena (*grandly*) I am Halloweena! The wickedest witch in the world!
Johnnie No, you're not. You're a [topical personality] look-a-like!

He and Susie laugh. So does the Cat!

Halloweena What are your names?
Johnnie That's for us to know and you to find out! Come on, puss. (*He takes Cat's paw*) We're taking you home with us.
Susie (*taking the other paw*) Yes. We'll be looking after you from now on.

They take Cat to DL *exit*

Halloweena moves to C. *The Cat stops and blows a raspberry at Halloweena*

Cat, Johnnie and Susie exit DL

Fit and Mabel enter from DR, *just in time to see them leave*

Fit There they are ... *together!*
Abel Let's get after them!

They start to rush across. Halloweena steps out in front of them. At the sight of her, the Duo pull up short with a terrified yell

Fit Who are you?
Halloweena I am your worst nightmare! (*She gives a fiendish laugh*) Ha! Ha! Ha! I am Halloweena! The wickedest witch in the world! I demand your assistance! Tell me the names of the two who just went out.
Fit Why d'you want to know?

Halloweena (*snarling*) That's *my* business! Tell me!
Fit (*to Mabel*) D'you think we should?
Mabel I'm not sure. (*To the audience*) What do you think, kids? Should
we tell her?
Audience No!
Halloweena (*to the audience*) Oh, yes, they should!
Audience Oh, no, they shouldn't! (*This continues ad-lib*)
Halloweena *Enough!* (*To the Duo*) Tell me their names, or ... (*menacingly*)
I will work my most diabolical magic on you!
Fit Oh, come on! There's no such thing as magic.
Mabel Or witches! Or dreadlocks!
Fit (*correcting her*) Warlocks!
Mabel (*pouting*) There's no need to speak to me like that!
Halloweena Are you questioning my magical power?
Duo (*with bravado*) Yes!
Halloweena Then a demonic demonstration is called for!

*She moves to one side and melodramatically prepares to summon the
evil forces. Sinister music plays under*

Mabel (*nervously*) What shall we do?
Fit Just humour her. I expect she's from [local place]!
Halloweena   I summon the powers of sorcery!
                      Come to my aid and work for me!
                      Show these doubters my true magic power!
                      Show them why they have cause to cower!
                      By the force of demons, hobgoblins and imps!
                      Change this pair into a couple of chimps!

She makes a magic pass at Fit and Mabel

*There is a flash. Fit and Mabel are immediately affected and take on
the comical characteristics of a pair of chimpanzees. They gibber and
scamper about. They groom themselves and each other. They even
leave the stage and go down into the audience to carry on their comic
capers. Sitting on laps, grooming, etc. etc. This continues ad-lib until
Halloweena calls an end to it*

                      Enough with Tarzan and his mate!
                      Return this pair to their normal state!

She makes a magic pass at Fit and Mabel

*There is a flash. Fit and Mabel are immediately back to normal. They
are confused and embarrassed to find themselves in the audience*

Fit (*sitting on a female lap*) What's going on? Who are you? Put me
down!
Mabel (*sitting on a male lap*) How did I get here? Oi! Keep your hands
off him! He's mine!

With comic business and ad-lib, they return to the stage

Halloweena Now do you believe I have magical powers?
Duo No!
Halloweena I changed you into a pair of monkeys!
Duo Oh, no, you didn't!
Halloweena Oh, yes, I did! (*Indicating the audience*) Ask them!
Duo (*to the audience*) Did she?
Audience Yes!
Duo Did she *really?*
Audience Yes!
Duo (*in horror*) Oh, no!
Halloweena So! Tell me their names, or I will change you into
something much worse!
Fit Johnnie Blue! Sometimes known as Little Boy Blue.
Mabel And Susie Sidebottom! Sometimes known as ... Susie
Sidebottom.
Halloweena (*rubbing her hands with devilish glee*) Excellent! Hee!
Hee! Hee!
Fit What are you gonna do to them?
Mabel I hope it's not something nasty!
Halloweena (*snarling at them*) Get out, before I change you into
[football team] supporters!
Duo (*wailing*) Oh, no! Anything but that!

Fit and Mabel run out DL

Halloweena (*to the audience, laughing*) Ha! Ha! Ha! So! Now that I
know their names I can take my revenge on that presumptuous pair of
pipsqueaks! Little Boy Blue and Susie Sidebottom are in for a nasty
surprise! A very nasty surprise! They will regret being rude to me! No
one does that to Halloweena and gets away with it! *No one!* (*Laughing
fiendishly*) *Ha! Ha! Ha!*

Laughing her evil laugh, Halloweena sweeps out DL

The Lights fade to black-out

Music to cover the scene change, and then the Lights come up on —

SCENE 3

The Grand Fête

Full set. The side wings represent colourful tents and stalls. Flags and bunting

The backcloth shows sky and picturesque countryside. Back C is a small rostrum. Up L is a sign pointing to off L and reading "BALLOON RIDES THIS WAY" Entrances R and L and at the back

The Stallholders are discovered setting up their stalls and tents. The Townsfolk enter from various directions and gaze about in wonderment. This develops into a lively song and dance

Song 6

After the number, Bessie bounces on from R. She is ludicrously dressed up for the fête

Bessie (*greeting the Townsfolk*) Hello, everybody!
Townsfolk Hello, Bessie!
Bessie (*spotting the audience and greeting them*) Hi, folks! You're still 'ere then? Must be rainin' out. (*Displaying her costume*) What d'you think of this little number? (*She does a twirl*) Not bad, is it? I got it in [local shop]. They were sellin' it at a *knock-down* price. That's right! You've got to be *unconscious* to wear it! On the way here all the boys kept givin' me the eye. I don't know what they wanted me to do with it! Anyway, I think this outfit really does something for me, don't you? (*She preens herself*) Oh, yes! (*To someone*) And I can see it's doing something for you, young man. If *that* sticks out any further we'll have to put safety cones around it! (*Slight pause*) I've never seen such a whopping great tongue! Put it away! (*Confidentially*) I'll let you into a secret, girls. I'm only wearing this to attract that chap with the balloon. That Wiggles. I think he fancies me.

Wiggles enters from L

(*To the audience*) Ooh! It's him! (*To him, waving*) Yoo hoo! Over here! (*She strikes her idea of sexy pose*)
Wiggles (*moving to her*) I say! Are you all right?
Bessie Course I am!
Wiggles Only you look like you're in pain.
Bessie I'm displayin' my new outfit! (*Sticking out her chest*) What d'you think?
Wiggles Outstanding!
Bessie Thank you.
Wiggles It reminds me of something. Oh, yes! Did I tell you I once owned two hot air balloons?
Bessie (*literally deflated*) What a let down!
Wiggles It's awfully nice to see your regalia.
Bessie Oh! I didn't know it was showin'!
Wiggles That dress, it's so ... er ——
Bessie Charming?
Wiggles (*vaguely*) No, I don't think it's alarming at all. (*To a Stallholder*) I say. Isn't it time the fête got under way?
Stallholder We're waiting for the mayor. He has to do the official opening.
Bessie (*to Wiggles*) Our mayor's just like one of your balloons. Full of hot air!

A bell is heard ringing off R. *All react*

The Town Crier enters from R, *ringing his bell*

The others clear to the sides as the Town Crier makes his way to the rostrum. Once there, he stops ringing his bell

Look out! It's the horse whisperer!
Town Crier (*booming*) Oyez! Oyez! Oyez! Make way! Make way for His Worship the Mayor of Merrydale!

A fanfare is played

Full of pomp, the Mayor enters from R. *He is now wearing his official robe and hat*

Bessie [Current model], eat yer heart out!

The Townsfolk roar with laughter. Annoyed, the Mayor signals to the Town Crier. He rings his bell and this stops the laughter

Town Crier Three cheers for His Worship the Mayor! Hip! Hip!
Townsfolk Hurray!
Town Crier Hip! Hip!
Townsfolk Hurray!
Town Crier Hip! Hip!
Bessie Go away!

The Townsfolk roar with laughter. After giving Bessie an angry glare, the Mayor makes his way to the rostrum. He trips as he mounts the step and falls on to the rostrum. Bessie and the others roar with laughter. The Town Crier helps the Mayor to his feet. He rearranges his hat, etc.

Mayor (*addressing the crowd*) Citizens of Merrydale. I would like to welcome you all to this, our annual grand open air fête. Before I proceed to the official opening, I have a few words I would like to say. (*He takes from his pocket a list. A very long list!*)
Bessie Oh, no! He's gonna read us his bill from the off licence! Get on with it!

The Townsfolk agree with cries of "Yes! Come on! Get on with it! Hurry up!" etc. etc.

Mayor (*stuffing the list back into his pocket*) All right! All right! (*He clears his throat and addresses the crowd*) As the Mayor of Merrydale, it gives me enormous pleasure ——
Bessie I bet it does!
Mayor To declare this fête well and truly — *open!*
All (*cheering*) Hurray!

Music strikes up

   A troupe of colourful dancers run on

Song 7

A lively dance number. If desired, this can be accompanied by singing from the Townsfolk

After the number, the Townsfolk cheer and applaud. The dancers bow and run out. The fête now gets underway. The stalls and tents are open for business. The Townsfolk can drift in and out of the scene until otherwise stated. The Mayor leaves the rostrum and mingles with the crowd

   The Town Crier exits

Wiggles (*to Bessie*) I'd better get back to my balloon. They'll be queuing up for rides. Perhaps I can give you one later on.
Bessie Chance would be a fine thing!
Wiggles I beg your pardon?
Bessie I hope it goes with a swing!
Wiggles Yes ... well ... cheerio!
Bessie Ta ta!

Wiggles exits L

Bessie watches him go and then turns away. As she does so she bumps into the Mayor

Bessie Whoops! ... Sorry! (*She sees who it is*) Oh! It's only you, Your Washup! Eh! I want a word with you.
Mayor (*eager to leave her*) Make it quick! What is it?
Bessie I don't see your Susie here anywhere.
Mayor No.
Bessie And I don't see my Johnnie either.
Mayor No.
Bessie I wonder why that is? (*With mock horror*) Oh, no! You don't suppose they're somewhere — *together!*
Mayor That's not going to happen.
Bessie What d'you mean?
Mayor (*smugly*) I have taken precautions.
Bessie So have I. And it didn't work!
Mayor My two servants have orders not to let Susie out of their sight. They will follow her everywhere and stop her from seeing that worthless son of yours.
Bessie Ooo! That's vicious! You mouldy old ... Mayor, you!

Unseen by the Mayor, Fit and Mabel enter from R. *They huddle and converse*

Bessie sees them and reacts

Oh! (*To Mayor*) They follow her everywhere, do they?
Mayor Everywhere.
Bessie And never let her out of their sight?
Mayor Not for a single second.
Bessie I see. So what are they doin' over there — on their own?! (*She points to the Duo*)
Mayor Eh? (*He spins round and sees the Duo. He yells at them*) Oy! You two!

Duo (*seeing him and letting out a scream*) Ahhhhgh!!

They make a run for the exit R

Mayor (*roaring*) Stop!

The Duo freeze in mid flight

Come here!

The Duo very nervously approach the Mayor

Fit (*timidly*) Hello, Your Worship.
Mabel (*the same*) Hello, Your Worship.
Mayor Never mind that! Where's Miss Susie? I told you not to let her out of your sight. Where is she?
Fit W-We don't know!
Mabel We haven't seen them since ... Oh! (*She slaps her hand over her mouth*)
Mayor *Them?!* Did you say *them?*
Fit She meant *her!*
Mabel Yes! (*Weakly*) It just came out *them!*
Mayor (*advancing on them, threateningly*) Is Susie with Little Boy Blue?
Duo (*backing away*) Er ... er ...
Mayor (*roaring at them*) Answer me! Is she with Little Boy Blue?!
Duo (*a terrified yell*) Yes!
Mayor (*exploding*) DOH!! You incompetent clowns! What have you got to say for yourselves?
Fit We're a bit worried.
Mabel We hope that horrible woman doesn't find them!
Mayor Horrible woman? (*He looks at Bessie*)
Bessie Well, don't look at *me!* There are *other* horrible women, y'know! (*To the audience*) Wot am I sayin'!
Mayor (*to Duo*) What are you talking about? What horrible woman?

Suddenly, Halloweena sweeps on from L, *and strikes a melodramatic pose*

Duo (*pointing to Halloweena*) That one!

There is a flash of lightning followed by a loud clap of thunder. The lighting becomes dark and sinister

This brings all the Townsfolk back on stage. Wiggles enters with them

Halloweena (*laughing her evil laugh*) Ha! Ha! Ha!
Bessie Oh, it's [current personality] again!
Mayor (*to Halloweena*) Who are you?
Halloweena I am Halloweena! The wickest witch in the world! Ha!
Ha! Ha!
Bessie (*to the audience*) They all end up 'ere, y'know! (*To Halloweena*)
Look Halitosis, or whatever yer name is, apart from having terrible
dress sense, you're sufferin' from diffusions. There's no such thing
as witches.
Halloweena Oh, no? (*Pointing to Fit and Mabel*) Ask them!
Fit She's telling the truth!
Mabel She really is a witch! She changed us into monkeys!
Fit It's true! (*To audience*) Isn't it, folks?
Audience Yes!
Bessie (*to the audience*) She changed these two into a pair of monkeys?
Audience Yes!
Bessie How could you tell the difference?
Halloweena Enough of this! Where is Little Boy Blue and Susie
Sidebottom?
Mayor Why do you want to know that?
Halloweena I have something for them!
Bessie What is it?
Halloweena A CURSE! (*Laughing her fiendish laugh*) Ha! Ha! Ha!

All react

Tell me where they are! (*Threateningly, she advances on them*) *Tell
me!*
Bessie Never! (*Pushing the Mayor in front of her*) You can torture him
all you like, but I will never tell!
Halloweena (*snarling*) Where are they?
Mayor (*terrified*) I ... I don't know!
Bessie And even if he did, he'd rather die than tell you! I hope they're
miles away where you'll never find them!
Halloweena Ha! My magic works just as well at long distance! It will
reach them wherever they are! Ha! Ha! Ha!

*Laughing her evil laugh, she moves away to R and prepares to summon
the evil forces. Sinister music plays under*

I summon the powers of sorcery!
Come to my aid and work for me!

> Little Boy Blue, my vengeance is near!
> You and Miss Susie have cause to fear!
> Being rude to me was a bad mistake!
> Your lives a misery now I will make!
> You cannot repent or go in reverse!
> For on you both I place — *this curse!*

She makes a magic pass. There is a flash. A pause. Nothing seems to have happened

Bessie (*to Halloweena*) Nothing! I think your Duracell's run out!
Duo (*looking and pointing to* L *entrance*) Look!

All look in that direction

> *Johnnie and Susie enter from* L. *They have both turned completely blue in colour! Face, hands, hair and clothes! (See Costume notes). The Cat follows them on*

There is general consternation at the sight of them. The two young lovers are equally shocked and awestruck. They cannot believe their own eyes. They gape at themselves and at each other

Johnnie Susie!
Susie Johnnie!
Johnnie What's happened to us?
Susie How did we get like this?
Halloweena (*with triumphant laughter*) Ha! Ha! Ha! It is my curse on you both! My sweet revenge! Now you really are Little Boy Blue! Ha! Ha! Ha! So perish all who would offend Halloweena! The wickedest witch in the world! Ha! Ha! Ha!
Susie You can't leave us like this!
Johnnie Change us back at once!
Halloweena You will remain like this *forever!* Only *I* can remove the curse! And that I will *never* do! Ha! Ha! Ha!

She raises her arms. There is a flash, followed by a complete black-out. There are cries of confusion in the darkness

> *Halloweena exits*

When the Lights come up, Halloweena has vanished from the scene. The lighting is back to normal. All react

Bessie (*going to Johnnie*) Oh! My poor boy! Look at the state of yah!
You've been smurfed. Does it hurt?

Johnnie No. I don't *feel* any different at all.

Bessie (*to Susie*) And are you the same — all over? I mean ... er ... (*She
whispers in her ear*)

Susie As far as I know. I haven't had time to check.

Johnnie We were on our way back when it happened.

Mayor (*pushing Bessie aside and confronting Johnnie*) Johnnie Blue!
I hold you responsible for this! Just look at my daughter! This would
never have happened if she'd kept away from you!

Susie Don't blame Johnnie, Daddy!

Bessie No! She's just the way you've always wanted her. A true blue,
all the way through!

Mayor (*to Johnnie, fuming with rage*) Listen to me! If you don't sort
this mess out I'll have you arrested and put in jail!

Bessie You can't do that!

Mayor Just you watch me!

Johnnie But how *can* I sort it out? You heard what the witch said. Only
she can remove the curse.

Mayor Then you'll have to *make* her remove it!

Susie But she's gone. Disappeared! We don't know where to find her.

The Cat pulls at Susie's dress, trying to attract her attention

What's the matter, puss?

Cat (*pointing to herself*) Meow! Meow!

Johnnie I think she's trying to tell us that she knows where to find the
witch. (*To Cat*) Is that right, puss?

Cat (*nodding*) Meow! Meow!

Bessie (*to the Audience*) Cor! It's wonderful stuff that Whiskas! (*Or
other cat food*) I'll have to try it!

Johnnie (*to Cat*) Is she very far away?

Cat (*nodding*) Meow!

Johnnie Across mountains?

Cat (*nodding*) Meow!

Johnnie Across seas?

Cat (*nodding*) Meow!

Johnnie (*despairingly*) Then it's hopeless! I'm sorry, Susie. I haven't
got the means to find the witch.

Wiggles (*coming forward*) But *I* have! Young man, my hot air balloon
is completely at your disposal.

Johnnie Do you mean it?

Wiggles Yes. We'll find that witch and get you two back to normal. Can you navigate and show us the way, puss?

Cat (*nodding*) Meow! (*She salutes Wiggles*) Meow!

Wiggles Jolly good!

Johnnie (*shaking Wiggles by the hand*) Thank you.

Susie Thank you. (*She hugs Wiggles*)

Bessie (*to Wiggles, elbowing Susie out of the way*) Well! It looks like you'll be givin' me that ride after all.

Johnnie Does that mean you're coming with us, Mum?

Bessie Try and stop me, lad! What about you, Mr Mayor?

Mayor Well ... I ... er ...

Bessie Not scared are yah?

Mayor (*hastily*) I have too many commitments. I'll be sending Fit and Mabel in my place.

Duo (*aghast*) What?!!

Mayor (*glaring at them*) To make sure nothing happens to Miss Susie!

Johnnie Then what are we waiting for? Let's go!

Bessie All we need is a stirring song to send us on our way!

Song 8

A stirring song and march for everyone

The music continues as Wiggles and Bessie march out L. They are followed by Johnnie and Susie with the Cat. Fit and Mabel follow next

A few seconds later, Fit and Mabel enter and make a run for the opposite exit. The Mayor heads them off and chases them out L

Excitedly, the Children point to off L. All the Townsfolk gather to look and point. Gradually they turn to face the back and we see the balloon drift into sight from off up L. (See Production Notes) The Townsfolk and Children wave as the balloon drifts across and out of sight up R

The Lights fade to black-out

Music to cover the scene change, and then the Lights come up on —

SCENE 4

The Witch's Lair

Tabs, or a front cloth showing the interior of a spooky cave with bizarre wall paintings. Entrances DR *and* DL

Weird lighting and strange sounds fill the air. A group of small Demons run on. To suitably sinister music they perform their demonic dance

Song 9

After the number, the Demons fall to their knees and bow towards the DL *entrance*

Laughing her evil laugh, Halloweena sweeps on from DL

Halloweena (*moving to* C) Ha! Ha! Ha!

At a gesture, she dismisses the Demons. They scuttle out DR *and* DL. *Halloweena turns her attention to the audience and receives the usual barrage of abuse*

(*Snarling at them*) Grr! You're *still* here, I see! And just as ugly and horrible!

By-play with the audience

Bah! You'd better start showing me some respect or you'll end up like Little Boy Blue and that stupid girlfriend of his! Bright blue, all over! Ha! Ha! Ha! I certainly got my revenge on that pair, didn't I? They will have to stay that colour forever! Only *I* can remove the curse! And those fools will *never* find me! Oh, no, they won't!
Audience (*correcting her*) Oh, yes, they will!
Halloweena Oh, no, they won't!

This continues ad-lib

Well, I don't believe a word you little creeps say! (*Picking on someone*) Especially you!
Squawker (*off* DL, *squawking loudly*) Squawk! Squawk!
Halloweena That sounds like ...? (*Looking to* DL) Yes! It is!

Squawker, an enormous (Man/Woman size!) bird hops on from DL. *It looks comically repulsive*

Squawker Squawk! Squawk!
Halloweena (*to the audience*) This is Squawker! My fine-feathered familiar!

Squawker hops across the front, peering at the audience with its head on one side

Squawker Squawk! Squawk! (*Talking, albeit with an awful croak*) Who are they, mistress?
Halloweena They need not concern you, Squawker. They are nothings! Mere worms!
Squawker (*getting excited and flapping its wings*) Worms! Squawk! *Worms!*
Halloweena Not *that* sort of worm, you feathered fool! (*Having an evil thought*) Although, I may let you have a peck at them later, if you're good. Now, tell me, what are you doing here?
Squawker I have something to report, mistress. Squawk!
Halloweena What is it?
Squawker Squawk! You're not going to like it!
Halloweena (*advancing on the bird, threateningly*) Tell me! Or must I fetch the sage and onion!
Squawker (*scared*) Squawk! It concerns Little Boy Blue!
Halloweena Little Boy Blue! What of him?
Squawker He and others are on their way here now! Squawk!
Halloweena (*greatly alarmed*) What?! On their way here! How do you know this?
Squawker I saw them! Squawk! They are in a balloon!
Halloweena A balloon!
Squawker Yes, mistress! Squawk!
Halloweena There is no time to be lost! Seek out this balloon! And with your beak and talons — *rip it asunder!*
Squawker (*very pleased*) Squawk!
Halloweena Send it plunging from the skies!
Squawker Squawk!
Halloweena And destroy them all!
Squawker (*excitedly flapping its wings*) Squawk! Squawk! Squawk!
Halloweena Stop that revolting moulting! (*Commanding*) *Fly!*

Flapping its wings and revving up, Squawker takes a run at the wings and exits DL

(*Sneering at the audience*) So! They are coming after me in a balloon, are they? (*With an evil chuckle*) Hee! Hee! Hee! Well, I wonder how they will like ballooning — without a balloon! We shall soon see! Ha! Ha! Ha!

Laughing her evil laugh, she sweeps out DL

The Lights fade to black-out or—

If more time is required for the scene change, the Demons can return and perform a short reprise of their dance

Reprise of Song 9 (Optional)

After the dance, the Demons rush out DR *and* DL *as the Lights fade to black-out*

Music to cover the scene change. This merges into something suggesting "up in the clouds", and the Lights come up on —

SCENE 5

Up in the Air

Half set. The backcloth shows blue sky and fluffy white clouds. The side wings represent sky and clouds. A ground row of clouds extends across the stage. In the centre, behind the ground row, is the basket of the balloon. Ropes stretch upwards, but the actual balloon is out of sight. (See Production Notes) In the basket are: Wiggles and the Cat, studying a chart. Johnnie and Susie, looking over one side. Fit and Mabel, looking over the other side. Bessie is nervously holding on to the ropes with her eyes tightly shut

Bessie Are we there yet? (*A pause*) Are we there yet?
Wiggles Hardly. We've still got a long way to go. (*To the Cat*) Isn't that right, puss?
Cat (*nodding*) Meow! Meow!
Bessie (*groaning*) Oooh!
Susie Why don't you open your eyes and take a look, Bessie?
Johnnie Yes, Mum. The view from up here is absolutely stunning.
Bessie It'd be even more *stunning* if I fell out and landed on me nut!
Wiggles You're not going to fall out. Not while I'm here. (*He puts a protective arm around her waist*)

Bessie (*snuggling against him*) Ooooo! You amorous aviator, you!
Wiggles Now, are you going to open them up for me?
Bessie (*indignantly*) I beg your pardon?!
Wiggles Your eyes. Come on. There's absolutely nothing to be afraid of.
Bessie Oh, all right! (*She slowly opens her eyes and looks straight out front. She is pleasantly surprised*) Ooo! It's not so bad after all! (*Pointing to the audience*) Look at all them fluffy clods!
Wiggles Don't you mean clouds?
Bessie I know what I mean! (*She sniffs and holds her nose*) Pooh! Are we passin' over [local place]?
Johnnie That was ages ago, Mum. We're passing over somewhere quite different now.
Wiggles (*pointing over the side*) Look!

Bessie looks down. She lets out a panic-stricken scream, staggers back and grabs hold of Wiggles. This causes the basket to rock about. The others cling to each other and stagger from side to side

Johnnie Watch out, Mum!
Fit You'll tip us out!
Wiggles Steady! Steady!
Bessie Oooh! I wanna get out!
Johnnie You're all right, Mum. Calm down.
Bessie Calm down he says! Me whole life flashed before me! All twenty-five years of it! Oh! I don't like it up 'ere! Let me get out! I'll catch a bus!
Johnnie That's impossible, Mum. We can't stop now. You'll be all right.
Susie Yes. You've just got a touch of vertigo.
Bessie (*wailing*) Ooooh!
Mabel D'you know what I do when I get scared?
Bessie Yes! And it'd be very thoughtless in a confined space like this!
Mabel I sing!
Bessie Oh!
Susie That's a good idea! It'll take your mind of things.
Fit What shall we sing?
Bessie Anything but *I'm Falling For You*! (*Or other suitable song*)
Johnnie We need something everyone knows.
Mabel What about [name of chosen song]?
Fit That's a good one!

Song 10

They sing and encourage Bessie to join in. They even call on the audience to help with the responses

Eventually, Bessie overcomes her reticence and sings along with them

Johnnie (*after the song*) Our friends sang very well, didn't they, Mum?
Bessie Compared to what? The mating call of the lesser-spotted bullfrog?
Susie Are you feeling better now?
Bessie A bit. I haven't got that verdigris anymore.
Susie That's good.
Bessie No. (*Indicating the audience*) They've given me earache instead!

The others laugh

> *Unseen by them, Squawker enters at the back. Flapping its wings to simulate flight, it moves about behind the basket*

The audience will start shouting out warnings

Johnnie (*to the audience*) What's wrong?
Audience Behind you!
Johnnie (*to the audience*) Pardon?
Audience Behind you!
Bessie (*to the audience*) Behind us? Is there something behind us?
Audience Yes!
Bessie Are you sure?
Audience Yes!
Bessie (*to the others*) I think there's something behind us!
Wiggles Perhaps we'd better look.
Bessie Right! On the count of three!
All One! ... Two! ... *Three!*

As they count, Squawker flaps out at the back

On "Three!" they all turn round to look at the back. Of course there is nothing to be seen

There's nothing there!

They all turn to face front again

> *Squawker returns at the back*

The audience shout out. The routine is repeated. Finally, when Squawker is still on stage, Bessie gets the others into a huddle

Bessie Y'know what we're doing wrong? We're counting out loud! We should whisper it.
All (*in a stage whisper*) One! ... Two! ... Three!

They all turn and see Squawker. All react at the sight of the huge bird

Bessie Crikey! What *is* that?!
Johnnie It's a giant bird!
Wiggles Has it spotted us?
Bessie I think it'll do more than *spot* us!
Squawker (*furiously flapping its wings*) Squawk! Squawk!

Squawking loudly, the giant bird "flies" in and out as it attacks the basket from both sides

Susie It's trying to attack us!
Wiggles (*to the bird*) I say! Do you mind clearing off?!
Bessie (*wafting the bird away*) Go away! Shoo! (*To Cat*) A fine moggy you are! Go on! See it off!
Cat (*at the bird, timidly*) Meow!
Squawker (*at the Cat, anything but timid*) Squawk! Squawk!

Scared, the Cat hides behind Bessie. Squawker comes in for another attack

Wiggles Don't let it get near the balloon! It'll puncture it!
Johnnie If only we had something to scare it away!
Bessie (*pointing to the audience*) Like their singin', y'mean?
Mabel That's it! (*To the audience*) Come on, folks!
Fit (*to the audience*) Yes! Let's get singing and frighten this big budgie away!
Mabel (*to the audience*) And as loud as you can this time!

Reprise of Song 10

They sing as loudly as they can and encourage the audience to do the same

The noise causes Squawker some distress. Seemingly out of control, it flaps about and eventually exits at the back

Johnnie signals for everyone to stop singing and they look about

Johnnie Has it gone?
Susie I think so.

Bessie (*to the audience*) *Has* it gone, folks?
Audience Yes!
Fit Are you sure?
Audience Yes!
Mabel Are you really *really* sure?
Audience Yes!
All Great!

But Squawker returns with a vengeance!

The cast and audience resume the loud singing

Eventually, Squawker is driven away for good

Bessie It's finally gone!
All (*to the audience, waving*) Thanks, folks!

Suddenly, the evil laughter of Halloweena is heard on an off stage microphone. At the same time, the lighting becomes dark and sinister. All react

Halloweena (*from an off stage mike*) Ha! Ha! Ha! So! You managed to scare away my feathered friend! Well, here is something you *won't* be able to scare away! Ha! Ha! Ha!
Bessie Oh, no! What's she up to now?

Halloweena's voice is heard again as she casts her spell. Sinister music plays under

Halloweena (*from off stage mike*) I summon the powers of sorcery!
Come to my aid and work for me!
Make thunder roar and lightning flash!
Make tempest howl and torrents lash!
Bring forth a storm, a mighty typhoon!
And rid me of this wretched balloon! Ha! Ha! Ha!

A storm to end all storms breaks out. Lightning flashes, thunder roars, howling winds, lashing rain. The works! The basket appears to be tossed about in the wind. (See Production Notes) Its occupants cling to each other and cry out in terror and panic. Loud, tempestuous music adds to the mayhem, as does Halloweena's continued laughter. When the pandemonium is at its height —

— the CURTAIN *falls*

ACT II

Somewhere in the Himalayas

Full set. The backcloth shows sky and snow-capped mountains and glaciers. The side wings and ground row represent snow-covered rocks and boulders. There is a large rock back C. *(The Yeti is concealed behind this) Entrances* R *and* L *and at the back*

Special lighting with falling snow effect. To suitable music, the fur-clad Himalayan Natives enter from various directions. When they have assembled, they go into their song and dance

Song 11

After the number, the storm conjured up by Halloweena suddenly strikes. Thunder and lightning, howling winds, blizzard, etc. The Natives react and huddle together

At the back, the balloon appears. It is being tossed about in the storm. (See Production Notes) Eventually, it is blown out of sight

The storm subsides. The Natives come out of their huddle and gaze about. A low growling is heard at the back. The Natives react and freeze, facing front. Slowly, from behind the rock at the back, the huge white shaggy figure of the Yeti rises into view. It climbs on to the rock and raises its arms. It lets out a tremendous roar

Slowly, the terrified Natives turn and see the Yeti. It waves its arms and lets out another roar

Natives *(yelling with fright)* YETI!! YETI!!

With panic-stricken screams, the Natives run out in various directions

The Yeti leaves the rock and lumbers forward. It becomes conscious of the audience and peers out at them. It gives a few roars and growls

Bessie (*off* R, *calling*) Yoo hoo! Johnnie?! Where are yooou?!

Hearing this, the Yeti quickly lumbers to the back and hides behind the rock

Bessie enters from R. *She is looking bedraggled and is shivering with the cold*

(*Still calling, between shivers*) Brr! ... Johnnie?! ... Brr! ... W-w-where are yah? ... Brr! (*She comes forward and spots the audience*) Oh! Hello, folks! You're 'ere as well, are yah? Brr! Cold init?! Brr! (*She shivers and business with dress*) Talk about frozen assets! I shall end up like our Johnnie at this rate! *Blue all over!* Brr! I suppose you're wonderin' what happened and how I got 'ere. Well, when that nasty witch gave us wet and windy in all areas, the balloon threw a wobbly and took a dive! Just as we were about to crash, I jumped out of the basket. Fortunately, the ground broke my fall. I landed right up to me neck in snow and ice! Brr! It's got into places I didn't know I had! (*She wriggles about*) Ugh! I feel as if I've got icicles as big as tricycles! When I crawled out I was all on me own! (*Getting tearful*) I don't know where I am or what's happened to Johnnie and the others! I'm just a poor little lamb who's lost in the snow! (*Wailing and crying*) Waaaah!

Wiggles (*off* L, *calling*) Hello?! Anyone there?!

Bessie (*misery forgotten and yelling*) Oi! Over 'ere!

Wiggles enters from L. *He too is looking bedraggled*

Wiggles!

Wiggles Bessie!

They rush into each other's arms and hug

Bessie *Ahhgh!* Don't hug too hard! I'm frozen stiff and you might break something off!

Wiggles I'm awfully glad you're safe, Bessie. Where are the others?

Bessie That's just what I was gonna ask you!

Wiggles You're the first person I've seen since I jumped out of the basket.

Bessie Same 'ere! (*Panicking*) Johnnie! What's happened to him? My poor boy! Oooh!

Wiggles Now, now. There's no need to panic. (*He puts a comforting hand on her shoulder*)

Bessie Oh, I'm in a bigger panic than that! (*She pulls his arm around her*) Oh! My poor son!

Wiggles I'm sure he's safe.

Bessie Where are we anyway?

Wiggles I'm not sure. That storm knocked us way off course. I have a feeling ——

Bessie You're lucky! I can't feel anything in this cold! (*Snuggling closer*) Per'aps you can try warmin' my cockles!

Wiggles I think we're in the Himalayas.

Bessie Eh? The Hima*where*ayas?

Wiggles The Himalayas. A mountain range in southern Asia. Y'know, Tibet, Mount Everest, and all that.

Bessie Never mind auditionin' for *Eggheads*! Are we safe here?

Wiggles Oh, yes! Perfectly safe. As long as we don't —— (*He breaks off*)

Bessie As long as we don't *what*?

Wiggles It's nothing.

Bessie (*nudging him in the ribs*) Tell me!

Wiggles As long as we don't encounter (*gulp*) it!

Bessie (*gulp*) It? What's (*gulp*) it?!

Wiggles (*with awe*) The abominable snowman!

Bessie (*scoffing*) A snowman! Surely you're not scared of a snowman! They've only got little twigs for arms! And they haven't got legs at all! What's a snowman gonna do? Poke us to death with its carrot nose?!

Wiggles It's not that sort of snowman. This is a huge white creature called the Yeti.

Bessie (*sarcastically*) Did you land on yer head when you jumped out of the basket?

Wiggles I'm only repeating what I've been told. The Yeti is probably just a myth. But many people claim to have seen it. And its giant footprints in the snow.

Looking at the ground, he moves away from her. He spots some "footprints" and follows them off stage L

Bessie (*to the audience, unaware that Wiggles has gone*) I've heard it all now! A snowman called Hettie! What a load of rubbish! Some people will believe anything! You don't believe in this Yeti, do yah?

Audience Yes!

Bessie Oh, come on! I expected better from you!

At the back, the Yeti rises from behind the rock. The audience will start shouting out warnings. The Yeti emerges and creeps up behind the oblivious Bessie

Audience Behind you!
Bessie Oh, no, you don't!
Audience Behind you!
Bessie I suppose you're gonna say it's the Yeti!
Audience Yes!
Bessie Well, you can't catch me out! There's no such thing and there's nothing behind me! Oh, no, there isn't!
Audience Oh, yes, there is!

This routine continues. During it, the Yeti moves to the right of the unsuspecting Bessie

Wiggles returns from L. *He is still looking at the ground and following the "footprints". He moves to the left of Bessie*

Bessie (*to Wiggles*) That lot are trying to make out there's something behind us.
Wiggles (*peering at the ground*) Hmm?
Bessie I said ... What are you looking at?
Wiggles These huge footprints. They're all over the place. Look.
Bessie Eh? (*She bends over to look at the ground*) Oh, yes! Cor! Must be somebody with whoppin' great wellie warmers!

Over her back Wiggles sees the Yeti standing there

He gives a "silent scream" and runs out L

The Yeti moves behind Bessie and stands on her left

(*Straightening up and facing front*) Hey! You don't think they belong to Hettie, the Yeti, do yah? (*Trembling*) Ooh! You've got me frightened now! Wiggles, let me hold your hand so I won't be so scared! (*Without looking she grabs the Yeti's paw and holds it tightly*) Oh! That's better! (*She strokes the hairy paw*) I think you could use some Veet (*or other hair-removing product*) though! And a visit to [local beauty salon/nail bar] wouldn't hurt! (*She wraps the Yeti's arm around her and snuggles up*) Mmmm! That's nice! I don't know where you got this fur coat from, but it's lovely and warm! (*She rubs her face against the hairy arm and shoulder*) Mmmm!

She looks up into the face of the Yeti. She shuts her eyes, and looks again. She looks to the audience and then back to the Yeti. In mute terror, she slides her body away from the creature

The Yeti moves towards Bessie, holding out its paws and growling. Bessie screams at the top of her lungs

Pursued by the Yeti, she runs around the stage and out R

Johnnie (*off* L, *calling*) Mum?! Wiggles? Where are you?!
Susie (*off* L, *calling*) Puss?! Fit and Mabel?! Are you there?!

Johnnie and Susie enter from L, *still calling and looking about*

Johnnie Mum? Wiggles?
Susie Fit and Mabel? Puss?
Johnnie There's not a sign of them anywhere.
Susie (*spotting the audience*) Look, Johnnie. Our friends are here.
Johnnie (*as they come forward to greet the audience*) So they are! Hello, folks!
Susie Hello! (*To Johnnie*) Perhaps *they* know what's happened to the others.
Johnnie (*to the audience*) Have you seen any of them?
Audience Yes!
Johnnie Who? Was it my mum?
Audience Yes!
Johnnie Good! Is she all right?

The audience explain about the Yeti, etc.

What's that? She's being chased by a *what*?
Susie A Yeti? What's a Yeti?
Audience A monster/creature!
Susie (*alarmed*) Oh, Johnnie!
Johnnie Don't worry. I pity any monster who chases *my* mum! So, like us she managed to escape the balloon.
Susie That means the rest did as well. All we've got to do is find them.
Johnnie (*despairingly*) And what will happen then? The balloon is wrecked. We can't get away from here. We'll never be able to find the witch now. I'm sorry, Susie. I got us into this awful mess and I can't get us out of it. (*Hanging his head*) It's all my fault!
Susie Cheer up. Don't be blue.
Johnnie (*with a half smile*) Is that supposed to be funny?

They both laugh and embrace

Susie And we're still together.

Johnnie And we always will be.

Song 12

A duet and dance. Suggestion: A song involving the colour blue. There is a suitable lighting change. This returns to normal after the number

Now, let's try to find Mum. (*To the audience*) Folks, did you see which way she was being chased?
Audience That way!
Johnnie (*indicating* R) This way? Great! (*To Susie, taking her hand*) Let's go! That poor Yeti might need our help!

Johnnie and Susie run out UR

A slight pause. Wiggles creeps on backwards from DL. *At the same time, Bessie creeps on backwards from* DR

In the centre their posteriors touch. Both yell and jump with fright. When they recognize each other, Bessie gives Wiggles a push

Bessie Ooo! You did give me a fright! I thought you were that abdominal snowman! That Yeti!
Wiggles Have you seen it?
Bessie Seen it! I nearly snogged it! It's been chasin' me all over the place!
Wiggles (*nervously*) Where is it now?
Bessie You're all right. I gave it the slip.

Unseen by them, the Yeti enters from R. *It creeps up behind the unsuspecting pair*

The audience will be shouting warnings

Wiggles (*to the audience*) What's wrong?
Audience Behind you!
Bessie Oh, no! Is it the Y-Y-Yeti?
Audience Yes!
Both (*in terror*) Oooo!!

They cling to each other and shiver and shake. The Yeti is right behind them

Wiggles (*to the audience*) Is it still there?
Audience Yes!
Bessie (*to the audience*) Are you sure?
Audience Yes!
Bessie (*to Wiggles*) I'm gonna look!
Wiggles Do you think that's wise?
Bessie Just do it!

Comic business as they nervously turn round with the Yeti keeping behind them

Bessie (*facing the back*) There's nothing there!
Audience Behind you!

Repeat turning business

Bessie (*facing the front*) There's still nothing there!
Audience Behind you!
Wiggles (*to the audience, moving away to one side*) Do you mind most awfully *not* playing tricks on us?
Bessie (*to the audience, moving away to the other side*) Yeah! Stop messin' about!

The Yeti stands between them

Wiggles You're making us very nervous! (*Without looking at her*) Aren't they, Bessie?
Bessie (*without looking at him*) Yes, they are. I need a cuddle!
Wiggles So do I!

Without looking they move towards each other. Needless to say it's the Yeti they both cuddle! Puzzled, they look at the creature and then do a huge "double take". Yelling with fright, they run out each side. The Yeti looks from right to left. It turns to the audience, gives a shrug and then lumbers out at the back

Fit and Mabel enter nervously from L. *They are being followed by a group of Natives. They are not aggressive, just curious. The Cat enters nervously from* R. *It is being followed by another group of curious Natives*

Duo (*seeing the Cat*) Puss!
Cat (*seeing them*) Meow!

They join each other at c. *The Natives close in around them*

Mabel (*clinging to Fit and looking nervously at the Natives*) We're being surmounted! What are we gonna do?
Fit I know! A cunning plan!
Mabel Yes?
Fit That's what we need, a cunning plan!
Mabel You're a man, think of something!

Fit whispers in her ear

(*Giving him a push*) Not that sort of something!
Fit (*after another look at the Natives*) They don't *look* aggressive, do they?
Mabel We said that about [local place]! And remember what happened there?
Fit Shall I gesticulate?
Mabel Not in front of them!
Fit I'll try talking to them.
Mabel Go on then.
Fit (*to the Natives, very slowly and loudly*) Hello! Nice to meet you! Lovely weather for the time of year!

The Natives look at each other, nonplussed

Mabel That worked well!
Fit I can't help it. I'm not bifocal! You try.
Mabel (*to the Natives, very slowly and loudly*) Hello! How do you do. Do you come here often?

Again the Natives look at each other, nonplussed

Cat (*holding up a paw*) Meow! Meow!
Mabel Do you want to try, puss?
Cat (*nodding*) Meow! Meow!

The Cat comes forward and signals to the conductor/Pianist. Music starts

Song 13

The Cat starts dancing. The Natives become interested

Fit Why didn't we think of that?

The Duo start singing and dancing. The Cat draws one of the Natives into the dance. Fit and Mabel do likewise. Very soon everyone is singing and dancing together

After the number, the Duo and the Cat shake hands with the Natives

  Johnnie and Susie enter from R

Susie (*seeing them*) Fit and Mabel!
Duo (*seeing her*) Miss Susie!
Johnnie Puss!
Cat Meow!

  The Duo and the Cat rush across to R, *and greet Johnnie and Susie. The Natives back off at the sight of the newcomers*

Johnnie (*indicating the Natives*) But who are they?
Fit It's all right. We're all friends now.

The Cat brings some of Natives forward to shake hands with Johnnie and Susie

Johnnie (*to the Duo*) Have you seen my mum?
Mabel No. Or Wiggles.
Johnnie I wonder what could have happened to them?

  Yelling, Bessie and Wiggles run on from L

  Mum!
Bessie Johnnie!

Mother and son rush into each other's arms. Wiggles remains L

  Oh! Am I glad to see you! (*To others*) And the rest of yah! Oh! We've had a time of it! (*Going back to Wiggles* L) Haven't we, Wiggles?
Wiggles Rather!
Bessie We've been chased by an 'orrible great monster!
Wiggles It's called the Yeti!
Natives YETI! YETI!

  The Yeti enters from L

Positions at this point are — Bessie and Wiggles together L. *Johnnie, Susie, the Duo and Cat* R. *The Natives are across the back*

Everyone sees the Yeti, except for Bessie and Wiggles. It moves to behind them

Bessie (*to Natives*) That's right! Some say it's a myth, but I'd say it's more of a Mithter!
Johnnie Mum!
Bessie Don't interrupt yer mummy when she's talkin'. Now, I'll tell you what it looks like. It's ——
Johnnie Tall?
Bessie ⎫ (*together*) Yes.
Wiggles ⎭
Johnnie White?
Both Yes.
Johnnie Hairy?
Both Yes.
Johnnie Claws?
Both Yes.
Johnnie Fangs?
Both Yes.
Bessie 'Ere! How do *you* know?
Johnnie Because it's standing right behind you!
Both What?!

They turn and see the Yeti. With a yell, they run over to Johnnie and the others. The Yeti holds up its arms and roars. Everyone cowers. Slowly, the Cat leaves the group and approaches the Yeti

Susie (*warningly*) Puss! Don't ...!
Johnnie Come back, puss!

The Cat takes no notice and moves closer to the Yeti

Cat (*to Yeti*) Meow? ... Meow?

The Yeti bends over and peers at the Cat. There is recognition. It falls to its knees and opens its arms wide. The Cat rushes into the Yeti's arms and they fondly embrace

Bessie (*to the Audience*) David Attenbourgh, eat yer heart out!

With caution, Johnnie and the others move across

Johnnie Puss ...?

The Cat leaves the Yeti. It rises to its feet

   (*To Cat*) I take it you two know each other?
Cat (*nodding*) Meow!
Johnnie And ... and is it friendly?
Cat (*nodding*) Meow!

The Cat takes the Yeti by the paw and leads it over to the others. It shakes hands with Johnnie, and then with Susie. It holds its paw out to Bessie

Bessie (*cringing away*) No, thanks!
Johnnie Go on, Mum.
Bessie (*to the audience*) Shall I?
Audience Yes!
Bessie (*to someone*) You would! 'Ere goes! (*She tentatively holds out her hand*)

The Yeti shakes it very politely

   Oo! That's not so bad.

The Yeti suddenly grabs her and gives her a bear hug. All find this amusing. Bessie disentangles herself and hides behind Wiggles

Johnnie Puss, do you think your friend can help us get away from here?

The Cat turns to the Yeti. They proceed to converse in a series of meows, grunts, growls and gestures

Mabel What are they saying?
Fit How should I know? I'm not Dr Doolittle!

The conversation over, the Cat turns back to Johnnie

Cat Meow! Meow!
Johnnie Will he help us?
Cat (*nodding*) Meow!
Wiggles Does that include repairing my balloon?

Yeti (*nodding*) Urgh! Urgh!
Bessie And finding that 'orrible witch?
Cat ⎱ (*together, nodding*) ⎰ Meow! Meow!
Yeti ⎰   ⎱ Urgh! Urgh!
Johnnie Then what are we waiting for?!
Bessie (*to Yeti*) Lead on, Mr Snowman!

Reprise of Song 13

All singing, they link hands and march around the stage

Led by the Yeti, they march out R, *waving to the Natives and the audience as they go*

The Natives wave and continue singing. Finally, we see the balloon drift into view at the back. The Natives turn upstage and wave to it. The balloon gradually drifts out of sight, as the Lights fade to black-out

"Flying" music to cover the scene change. This changes to something suitably sinister as the Lights come up on —

SCENE 2

The Witch's Lair

As ACT I, SCENE 4

Weird sounds and spooky lighting

Reprise of Song 9 (Optional)

NOTE: If more time is required for changing into the next scene, the Demons can perform a reprise of their dance number from ACT I SCENE 4. *If used, they exit afterwards*

Halloweena sweeps on from DL. *She is met with the usual barrage of abuse from the audience*

Halloweena (*snarling at the audience*) Grr! Are you disgusting specimens *still* here? I heard you had been arrested for making the place look untidy! Hee! Hee! Hee! Well, *you* may be still here but

Little Boy Blue and the other fools aren't! After the storm I conjured up they are all drowned or smashed to pieces! They will never trouble me again! Will they?

Audience Yes!

Halloweena Oh, no, they won't!

Audience Oh, yes, they will! (*This continues ad-lib*)

Halloweena You seem very sure of yourselves. Do you know something I don't?

Audience Yes!

Halloweena And are you going to tell me what that something is?

Audience No!

Halloweena (*snarling at them*) Grr! You're rubbish! What are you?

While the audience's attention is focused on Halloweena, Squawker enters at the back of the auditorium

Squawker (*loudly*) Squawk! Squawk!

The audience are now aware that Squawker is behind them

Halloweena (*peering out front and calling*) Squawker? Is that you?

Squawker Yes, mistress! Squawk!

Halloweena Come to me at once!

Squawker Squawk! Squawk!

The giant bird makes its way to the stage through the audience. Comic business and ad-lib as it causes havoc en route. Eventually, it mounts the stage and hops over to Halloweena

Squawker Squawk! Squawk!

Halloweena These fools know something concerning Little Boy Blue! But they won't tell me what it is!

Squawker (*to audience*) Squawk! Squawk!

Halloweena Do *you* know what it is, Squawker?

Squawker Yes, mistress! Squawk!

Halloweena You do?

Squawker Yes, mistress! Squawk!

Halloweena (*yelling*) Then tell me!!

Squawker You're not gonna like it! Squawk!

Halloweena (*threateningly*) Tell me! Or must I fetch the parsley and thyme?

Squawker Little Boy Blue and the others escaped the storm! Squawk!

Halloweena (*enraged*) What?

Squawker And that's not all! Squawk!

Halloweena What else?
Squawker They're on their way here — right now! Squawk!
Halloweena (*fuming*) Are they indeed? Grrrr!

Seething with rage, Halloweena paces up and down

Squawker (*to the audience*) That's really got up her beak! Squawk!

Halloweena stops pacing and turns with a malicious grin

Halloweena Well, let them come! I will have a surprise waiting for
them! (*With an evil cackle*) Hee! Hee! Hee!
Squawker (*hopping over to her*) Squawk! What is it, mistress?
Halloweena You will have to wait and see, Squawker! (*To the audience*)
And so will you! Suffice to say, it will *not* be a *pleasant* surprise! Hee!
Hee! Hee!

Squawker joins her with its version of an evil cackle

(*With relish*) Oh, I *love* being *evil*!
Squawker So do I, mistress! Squawk!
Halloweena Yes! It's nice to have a friend to share in the misery and
mayhem!

Song 14

A comedy "nasty" duet and dance for Halloweena and Squawker.

It ends with them performing a high stepping exit

Lights fade to black-out

Music to cover the scene change, and then the Lights come up on —

SCENE 3

Swamp on the Witch's Island

*Full set. A creepy scene. The backcloth shows the rest of the volcanic
island under a strange, multi-coloured sky. At the sides, gnarled trees
overhang the steamy swamp. Dense undergrowth and tangled creepers
abound. A reddish glow illuminates the scene and strange sounds fill the
air. Ground mist swirls*

After a pause, the balloon drifts into view at the back. (See Production Notes)

Still performing the dance steps from the previous number, Squawker struts on from L. *Eventually, it becomes aware of the balloon and excitedly hops up and down*

Squawker Squawk! Squawk! (*He hops to* L *and squawks to off stage*) Squawk! *Mistress! Mistress!*

Halloweena sweeps on from L

Halloweena What is it? (*She sees Squawker hopping about*) No! I refuse to dance anymore!
Squawker (*pointing its wing at the balloon*) Look, mistress! Squawk! Look!

Haloweena sweeps upstage to observe the balloon

Halloweena So! They are here! Like lambs to the slaughter! Ha! Ha! Ha!

The balloon drifts out of sight. Halloweena and Squawker rush to the side and watch its progress off stage

They are landing on the other side of the island! (*To Squawker*) Quick! Seek them out and observe their movements. (*Commanding*) Fly!
Squawker Yes, mistress! Squawk!

Frantically flapping its wings and revving up, Squawker takes a run at the wings and exits

Halloweena (*to the audience, moving forward*) Meanwhile, I will arrange the little surprise I have in store for Little Boy Blue! Ha! Ha! Ha!

Laughing demonically, she takes centre stage and prepares to summon the powers of darkness. Sinister music plays under

O, powers of darkness, I call on thee!
Come to my aid and work for me!
Ha! Ha! Ha!

There is a flash of lightning. This is followed by a great clap of thunder

The lighting becomes even more sinister and spooky. Halloweena moves to DL

>I summon my hideous and gruesome slaves!
>Come, my zombies! Rise from your graves!
>Fill all who see you with dread and fear!
>Come forth, my zombies! I command you — *appear!*

There is flash of lightning. This is followed by a great clap of thunder. More ground mist swirls

Suitable music plays as the gruesome Zombies make their jerky entrances. Some appear to rise out of the swamp at the back. Others shamble on from the sides. Perhaps a few can enter through the audience! Finally, they all converge on stage and go into their quirky song and dance number

Song 15

Song and dance for Zombies

After the number, the Zombies turn to Halloweena and give jerky bows

Zombies Urgh! Urgh!
Halloweena And it's nice to see you too, my flesh-eating friends. Welcome.
Zombies Hun-gry! Hun-gry!
Halloweena Ah! Feeling peckish, are you?
Zombies (*with jerky nods*) Urgh! Urgh!
Halloweena Good! Never fear. Your appetites will soon be satisfied.

This obviously pleases the Zombies

Squawker "comes in to land" from R. *It reacts on seeing the Zombies. They think dinner has arrived and stumble towards the bird, slavering and reaching out*

Zombies Urgh! Urgh! Urgh!
Squawker (*in terror*) Squawk! Mistress! Squawk!
Halloweena Stop!
Zombies (*obeying, but puzzled*) Urgh?
Halloweena *That* is *not* dinner!
Zombies (*disappointed*) Urgh!
Halloweena Have patience, my carnivorous companions! Very soon there will be plenty of *human* flesh for you to sink your teeth into!

Zombies (*pleased again*) Urgh! Urgh!
Halloweena (*crossing to Squawker*) What news of Little Boy Blue?
Squawker The balloon has landed! Squawk! He and the others are on their way here now! Squawk!
Halloweena (*with devilish glee*) Hee! Hee! Hee! Excellent! They are walking straight into my trap! Ha! Ha! Ha!

Squawker joins her in evil laughter. So do the Zombies!

(*To Zombies*) Dinner will be served shortly, my friends!
Zombies (*over the moon*) Urgh! Urgh!
Halloweena But first you must conceal yourselves and await my signal. Go!

The Zombies shuffle out in various directions. The lighting reverts to previous setting

(*To Squawker*) We must do likewise! (*To the audience*) Soon Little Boy Blue and his stupid friends will trouble me no more! They will be the main course on my zombies menu! And when they've finished that, I will serve you as dessert! Ha! Ha! Ha!

Laughing their evil laughs, Halloweena and Squawker exit L

After a slight pause, Bessie and Wiggles creep on from R. *They move forward, looking nervously about them*

Wiggles (*catching sight of the audience*) Ah!
Bessie (*jumping with fright*) Ahhgh! (*Clutching him in fear*) What is it?
Wiggles It's all right. It's only our awfully nice friends.
Bessie (*peering out at the audience*) So it is! Hello, folks!
Audience Hello!
Bessie (*to Wiggles*) It's funny, innit? Wherever we go, they get there first! (*To audience*) Guess what? We're lost again!
Wiggles (*to the audience*) I landed the balloon safely ...
Bessie And we all got out to explore ...
Wiggles When we turned round ...
Bessie All the others had gorn an' gorn! So, 'ere we are — *lost!* We can't even find our way back to the balloon! (*Turning on Wiggles*) A fine navigator you are!
Wiggles I'm awfully sorry. I've completely lost my bearings.
Bessie I thought you were walking a bit funny!
Wiggles So now we're absolutely lost!

Bessie (*looking about, with dread*) And what a place to be lost in! It's nearly as creepy as the [local pub/club] at closing time!
Wiggles (*hearing something*) Shh!
Bessie What?
Wiggles I heard a noise.
Bessie I can't help it. It's all this excitement!
Wiggles (*looking to* L) I ... I think it came from over there. (*He creeps towards* L)
Bessie Oh, be careful! Who knows what might lurk in the murk!
Wiggles Shh! I heard it again! There's definitely something here!

Slowly, Wiggles reaches off stage. He leads Fit on by the hand

Bessie Oh! Thank goodness!
Wiggles It's one of us!
Bessie You look like one of the others! Standin' there holding hands!

Fit and Wiggles drop hands

Fit Have you seen Mabel?
Bessie No, I ... Shh! I heard something! (*Moving to* R) I bet it's her! (*She reaches off stage*) Yes! Here she is!

Without looking, she leads Halloweena on by the hand!

Wiggles and Fit just gape

Mabel enters from L

Mabel Hello!

Bessie sees Mabel and does a huge double take. She looks at Halloweena. With a yell, she throws away the witch's hand and runs across to join the others on L

Halloweena Ha! Ha! Ha!

Squawker hops on from R

Squawker Squawk! Squawk!
Bessie Oh, no! It's that foul pest again!
Halloweena (*moving to* C) So! You are in my power! (*She reacts*) Ah! ... Where is Little Boy Blue?

Others We don't know!
Halloweena Where is Susie Sidebottom?
Others We don't know!
Halloweena You lie! Still, no matter! I will soon seek them out and
destroy them! (*To the audience*) No one can escape from Halloweena,
the wickedest witch in the world! Ha! Ha! Ha!
Bessie (*to the audience*) Thinks a lot of herself, doesn't she?
Halloweena But first, I must deal with you! Ha! Ha! Ha!

Halloweena sweeps to DR. *Squawker joins her*

> Come, my zombies! Rise from the slime!
> Come and get it! It's your dinner time!
> Ha! Ha! Ha!

*There is a flash of lightning. This is followed by a great clap of thunder.
The lighting becomes even more sinister and spooky. Ground mist swirls.
Strange sounds fill the air*

Bessie and the others cling to each other in terror

> *To suitable music, the Zombies emerge and shamble on from various
> directions*

Fit Oh, no! It's the [reference to local council]!
Zombies Hun-gry! Hun-gry!

*Bessie and the others form a terrified huddle in the centre as the Zombies
surround them*

Halloweena   Eat every scrap! To waste is a sin!
                     Don't leave a morsel! Get stuck in!

*Slavering and reaching out, the hungry Zombies advance on the
cowering group*

> *Suddenly, the Yeti enters from* DL

The lighting suddenly becomes much brighter

Yeti (*raising its arms and roaring*) ARRRRRRGH!!

> *The Zombies stagger backwards. Emitting frightened wails, they
> stumble out in various directions. This is the fastest they have moved!*

Halloweena (*to the Yeti, with recognition*) You?!
Yeti (*nodding*) Arrh!

Halloweena makes for the exit DR

Suddenly, the Cat enters DR *and prevents her escape*

It hisses and snarls at Halloweena, causing her to retreat to C

Halloweena (*cowering, obviously terrified at what is to come*) No! ...
No! ...

*The Yeti and the Cat both point at the witch and pronounce the magic
spell. It still sounds like a meow and a roar!*

Yeti }
Cat } (*together*) ABRACADABRA!!!

There is a blinding flash. This is followed by a complete black-out

Halloweena, Yeti and Cat exit

A Girl and Woman enter

*Strange sounds and magical music is heard. When the Lights come up,
the scene is much brighter and less sinister looking. The sounds and
music fade out. Halloweena has vanished from the scene. So has the Yeti
and the Cat! In place of the Yeti stands a beautiful woman, and in place
of the Cat, a pretty young girl. Both look ethereal and wear diaphanous
costumes. The Girl still wears the cat collar*

Woman Daughter!
Girl Mother!

*The Girl runs across into the Woman's arms. Completely dumbfounded,
Bessie and the others move down* C. *Squawker cowers away on* L

Fit I think we've wandered into a Harry Potter! (*Or something current
to suit*)
Bessie (*to Woman*) Er ... excuse me, luv? Wot's up?
Woman You are all quite safe now.
Wiggles Where's the witch?
Girl She has gone.
Woman Forever.

The others show great relief, expect for Squawker

Squawker (*squawking pitifully*) Mistress!
Bessie (*to Squawker*) Are you still here? I've got one thing to say to
   you — PAXO!!

Hysterically squawking and flapping its wings, Squawker exits R

Wiggles (*to Woman*) Hello. This is all terribly strange. Would you be
   awfully kind and elucidate?
Bessie Never mind that! Just ask 'er what the 'eck's goin' on?
Woman Allow me to explain. I —

Johnnie and Susie enter from R. *They are no longer the colour blue!*
Face, hands, hair and clothes are all back to normal

Johnnie Hello, everyone!
Bessie (*turning*) Johnnie! (*She rushes across to hug him and then notices
   their change of colour*) Hey! You're both back to normal! You're not
   blue anymore!
Johnnie I know! Isn't it wonderful?
Susie We were just walking along and it suddenly happened.
Johnnie We don't know how or why.
Bessie I think we're about to find out! (*To Woman and Girl*) Over to
   you, Ant and Dec!
Woman Thank you. To begin with, I am a *white* witch. That means I
   use my magic powers only for good. This is my daughter. She is also
   my apprentice. Some years ago we were called upon to rid a certain
   land of an evil witch.
Girl Halloweena!
Woman She proved to be a very formidable adversary.
Girl She used every dirty magic trick in the book!
Woman (*mildly reprimanding her*) Who's telling this fairy tale?
Girl Sorry, Mother.
Woman Before we could use our combined forces, Halloweena managed
   to separate us. It was then that she worked her most diabolical magic.
   She turned me into a creature that became known as the Yeti!
Girl And she turned me into a common cat!
Woman I was doomed to wander the snowy wastes forever!
Girl And she took me along with her as a pet!
Woman Separated, and in these forms, our magic powers diminished.
   We were helpless.
Girl It was not until you came along that things could be made right.

Woman Because of you I have been reunited with my daughter. And together we could defeat Halloweena. With her demise, all her evil curses have been lifted. Thus your return to your natural state.
Johnnie There's one thing I don't understand. How did ——?
Bessie (*aside to him*) Don't ask questions or we'll be 'ere all night! Just thank 'em and let's get out of 'ere.
Johnnie Thank you both very much.
Susie Yes, thank you.
Girl You showed me great kindness in my other life as a cat. For that I would to like you to accept this gift.

The Girl removes her collar and hands it to Johnnie. Bessie and the others gather round to look

Bessie (*awestruck*) Wow!
Johnnie Are those real diamonds?
Girl I believe they are.
Bessie *Wow!* Wot whoppers!
Susie They must be worth a fortune!
Bessie *Wow!* (*To the audience*) It's better than anything on *Flog It*!
Johnnie (*to the Girl*) What I did for you was out of friendship. (*He holds out the collar*) Thank you, but I can't accept this.
Bessie *EH?!*
Johnnie It's too much, Mum.
Woman With our magical powers we have no need of material wealth. Please accept the gift.
Bessie (*nudging Johnnie*) You 'eard her!
Johnnie (*unsure*) Well ...
Susie You'll be rich, Johnnie. My father will fall over himself to let us marry.
Johnnie That's true! (*To Woman and Girl*) Thank you. (*He puts the collar in his pocket or belt*)
Bessie (*over the moon*) Atta boy!
Woman I am sure you are all anxious to return to your homes.
All Yes!
Bessie 'Specially now we're rich! (*To the audience*) Oh! This'll be one in the eye for the [local reference]!
Woman Then we will detain you no longer. Come, daughter.

The Girl moves back to her mother

Woman }
Girl } (*together, waving*) Farewell!

There is a flash, followed by a complete black-out

The Woman and Girl exit

The Lights come up

Bessie Crikey! They didn't 'ang about! (*Having a sudden annoying thought*) Oh, bu ... blow!
Wiggles What's the matter?
Bessie They could have used their magic to get us 'ome! Now we'll have to go back by blinkin' balloon!
Wiggles It won't be so bad doing it a second time.
Bessie (*to the audience*) Where've I heard that before, girls?! (*To the others*) Come on then! Let's get goin'!
Fit Just a minute. Isn't there something we should do before we set off?
Bessie Don't be so personal! Anyway (*looking about*) I don't know where they are!
Mabel He means we always sing a song!
Bessie Oh, yes! You're right! (*Indicating the audience*) And they'd be ever so disappointed if we didn't! (*To audience*) Wouldn't you? (*By-play with audience*) Too bad, because you're gonna get it! (*To conductor/pianist*) Take it away, Sir Elton!

Song 16

A joyful song and dance for all. If practical, the Zombies could enter and join in. The number ends with a tableau, and the Lights fade to black-out

Music to cover the scene change, and then the Lights come up on —

Scene 4

Back home again. As ACT I Scene 2

Fit and Mabel enter from DR. *They greet the audience*

Fit Hello, folks!
Mabel Hi, kids!
Fit Well, we've been back home for a whole week now.
Mabel Doesn't time fly when you're enjoying yourself?
Fit With those diamonds, Little Boy Blue and his mum are the richest family in town.

Mabel They're even richer than [local reference]!
Fit Of course the Mayor's sucking up to them. The old creep!
Mabel He can't wait for his daughter and Johnnie to get married.
Fit Which they are — *next week!*
Mabel And that's not the only bit of romance. We're getting married next week as well! Aren't we, my snuggle puss?
Fit Yes we are, my little sweetie pie!

They hold hands and act all soppy

Mabel It'll be just like William and Kate!
Fit Only more so!

They comically cuddle and canoodle

  The Mayor enters from DL

Mayor Oi! You two!
Duo Hello, your worship!
Mayor Have you got a licence to do that in public?
Fit We can't help it, your worship.
Mabel No! We're in *luuuuuv!*

They resume their comic canoodling

Mayor (*disgusted*) Oh, stop it! (*But they continue*) You won't drive me away! (*Aside to the audience*) I haven't been on for ages, and I'm gonna make the most of it! (*Crossing and pulling them apart*) Break! I'm looking for Bessie Blue. Have you seen her?
Fit No. I expect she's gone to [local place]! Buying up all the clothes!
Mabel And shoes! (*She looks to off* DR) Oh! Here she comes now!

Fit and Mabel exit DL

Bessie enters from DR, *singing "We're in the Money". She is outrageously dressed to display her new found wealth. (See Costume Notes) She moves to* C, *and greets the audience with the royal wave*

Bessie (*ultra posh*) Greetings, peasants! Greetings! (*As herself*) Hello, folks! Hi, kids! I've just bin doin' a bit of shoppin'. (*She calls to* DR) In you come!

A long line of children enter from DR. *They are carrying shoe boxes, large packages and bulging carrier bags. They march across and exit* DL

(*To the audience*) Just a few things for the weekend! But money's not everything, y'know. I went to see about having a face lift. But when they saw what was underneath they let it drop again!

The Mayor sidles over to beside Bessie

(*Sensing him*) Oh-oh! I think summit's pitched!

Mayor (*very smarmy*) Hello, Bessie.

Bessie Oi! It's *Mrs Blue* to you! What d'you want? (*To audience*) I know what 'e's gonna *get!*

Mayor (*snuggling up to her*) I must say you're looking very alluring.

Bessie (*shrugging him off*) And you're lookin' for a thick ear!

Mayor I wonder if you'd care to accompany me to the cinema this evening. One of my favourite films is showing.

Bessie Starring Meryl *Creep*, no doubt! That's three times this week you've asked me to go out with yah! Not so long ago I was riff-raff! Not good enough to lick your boots! Now you can't get enough of me! I wonder why? Could it be something to do with my new found effluence?

Mayor (*blustering*) Oh, no ... I ... I've always admired you ... from afar.

Bessie Well, go and admire me from a lot further! Push off!

Mayor (*pleading*) Bessie! I appeal to you!

Bessie Oh, no, you don't!

Mayor I've always had a soft spot for you.

Bessie Yes, we can all see it! Well, it's no use, because ... (*Melodramatically*) My heart belongs to another!

Mayor What?!

Bessie So does my liver, my lungs and all my other bits!

Mayor Who is he?

Bessie (*with her hand to her brow*) I cannot speak his name!

Mayor Forget him! Come to me! Be my money ... er ... honey!

The Mayor grabs Bessie and tries to kiss her

Wiggles enters from DR

Wiggles (*viewing the scene*) Oh, I say!

Bessie Wiggles! This is not what it looks like! *Ger off!* (*She pushes the Mayor away and rushes to Wiggles*) I thought you'd gone and left me! Me, the richest babe this side of [local place]!

Wiggles Would you describe yourself as *filthy rich?*

Bessie No — just filthy! Ha! Ha! (*To audience*) That joke was first published in eighteen eighty-five! (*To Wiggles*) Come 'ere! (*She grabs Wiggles and hugs him tightly*)

Mayor (*stamping his foot*) DOH!

The Mayor stomps out DL

Bessie Does this mean you're askin' me to be your awful wedded wife?
Wiggles Well, I —
Bessie Because the answer's YES! (*She links arms with him*) Come on!
Let's go and see [local vicar] before you change yer mind! (*To the
audience*) Bye, folks! See you at the wedding! Bye!

Waving to the audience, Bessie and Wiggles exit DR

Fit and Mabel enter from DL, *greatly excited*

Mabel Another wedding! That makes three!
Fit Just think of all the stag and hen nights!
Mabel All the parties and receptions!
Fit All the singing and dancing!
Mabel (*artfully*) Talking of singing ...
Fit Oh, yes! Don't think we've forgotten you.
Mabel You're gonna get *your* chance — *right now!*

*The song sheet is lowered, or Fit and Mabel can fetch it from the wings.
Or two of the Chorus/Children can bring it on*

Fit You thought you'd got away with it, didn't you?
Mabel This is an easy one. We'll sing it once and then it's your turn.

Song 17

*Fit and Mabel have fun getting the audience to sing. If desired, the
house lights can go up and children are taken on stage. They are asked
their names and ages, etc. When they return to their seats, the song is
repeated. The Song Sheet is then removed.*

Fit and Mabel run off, waving goodbye to the audience

The Lights fade to black-out

Ringing his bell, the Town Crier enters. He is illuminated by a spotlight

Town Crier *Oyez! Oyez! Oyez!* Today three weddings will take place in
Merrydale! The marriages of Johnnie Blue and Susie Sidebottom, Fit

and Mabel, Willard Wigglesworth and Bessie Boadicea Blue! *Oyez!*
Oyez! Oyez!

Ringing his bell, the Town Crier exits

The spotlight is taken out

Wedding bells ring out. The Lights come up on —

SCENE 5

The Grand Finale

A special finale setting, or the town square set can be used with added decorations

Bright lighting and bouncy music. The whole company enter for the walk down and bows. The three couples are dressed for their wedding. (See Costume Notes) The last to enter are Johnnie and Susie, magnificently attired

Johnnie	Never again will I feel blue.
Susie	Nor will I, while I'm married to you.
Mabel	The fruits of love will be our bill of fare.
Fit	Please keep for me the biggest pear!
Wiggles	Are you looking forward to our honeymoon?
Bessie	As long as it's not in that blinkin' balloon!
Mayor	(*to the Witch*) Would you like to be my Mrs Mayor?
Halloweena	I'd rather spend time with Tony Blair! (*Or another name that rhymes*)
Cat	At times like this I'm glad I can't talk.
Squawker	You can say that again! Squawk! Squawk! Squawk!
Woman	We hope you have enjoyed the show.
Girl	The time has come for us to go.
Johnnie	So as we bid you a fond adieu,
	It's goodbye and god bless
All	(*waving*) From LITTLE BOY BLUE!

Song 18

Finale song or reprise

CURTAIN

FURNITURE AND PROPERTY LIST

ACT I

SCENE 1

On stage: Backcloth showing field with tents, stalls and a hot air balloon
Town Square wings
Town Hall entrance with steps

Off stage: Handbell, scroll (**Town Crier**)
Scrubbing brush, plastic bucket (**Bessie**)
Plastic bucket (**Mayor**)

SCENE 2

On stage: Tabs, or front cloth showing a country lane

SCENE 3

On stage: Backcloth showing sky and countryside
Tent wings
Stalls with dressing
Low rostrum
Flags and bunting
Sign reading "BALLOON RIDES! THIS WAY"

Off stage: Handbell, scroll (**Town Crier**)
Model hot air balloon (**Stage Management**)

SCENE 4

On stage: Tabs, or front cloth showing interior of a spooky cave

SCENE 5

On stage: Backcloth showing sky and clouds
Sky and cloud wings
Cloud ground row
Balloon basket with ropes and dressing

Off stage: Chart (**Wiggles**)

ACT II

Scene 1

On stage: Backcloth showing snow-capped mountains and glaciers
Snow covered rock and boulder wings
Ground row with large rock

Off stage: Model hot air balloon (**Stage Management**)

Scene 2

On stage: Tabs, or front cloth as ACT I, Scene 4

Scene 3

On stage: Backcloth showing swamp and island with strange,
multi-coloured sky
Swamp wings of gnarled trees and tangled creepers
Swamp ground row

Off stage: Model hot air balloon (**Stage Management**)

Scene 4

On stage: Tabs, or front cloth as ACT I, Scene 2

Off stage: Shoe boxes, packages, bulging carrier bags (**Children**)
Song sheet (**Fit** and **Mabel** or **Chorus/Children**)
Handbell (**Town Crier**)

Scene 5

On stage: Special finale setting or Town Square set can be used with
added decorations

LIGHTING PLOT

Various interior and exterior settings

ACT I, Scene 1

To open: General exterior lighting

ACT I, Scene 2

To open: General exterior lighting

| *Cue* 11 | End of Song 5 | (Page 15) |
| | *Return to previous setting* | |

| *Cue* 12 | **Halloweena** (*off*) "CAAAAT!!" | (Page 16) |
| | *Dark and sinister lighting* | |

| *Cue* 13 | **Fit** and **Mabel** enter the auditorium | (Page 18) |
| | *House lights up* | |

| *Cue* 14 | **Fit** and **Mabel** return to the stage | (Page 19) |
| | *House lights down* | |

| *Cue* 15 | **Halloweena** exits | (Page 19) |
| | *Fade to black-out* | |

ACT I, SCENE 3

To open: General exterior lighting

| *Cue* 16 | **Fit** and **Mabel**; "That one!" | (Page 24) |
| | *Flash of lightning. Dark and sinister lighting* | |

Cue 17	**Halloweena** raises her arms. There is a flash	(Page 26)
	Black-out. Allow time for **Halloweena** *to exit,*	
	and then return to previous general exterior lighting	

| *Cue* 18 | As the balloon drifts out of sight | (Page 28) |
| | *Fade to black-out* | |

ACT I, SCENE 4

To open: Weird interior lighting

| *Cue* 19 | **Halloweena** or **Demons** exit | (Page 31) |
| | *Fade to black-out* | |

ACT I, SCENE 5

To open: Bright general exterior lighting

Cue 20	**Halloweena** is heard laughing on an off stage	(Page 35)
	microphone	
	Dark and sinister lighting	

| *Cue* 21 | **Halloweena** "Ha! Ha! Ha! | (Page 35) |
| | *Violent storm effect. Flashes of lightning* | |

ACT II, SCENE 1

To open: General exterior lighting

Cue 22	End of Song 11 *Violent storm effect. Flashes of lightning*	(Page 36)
Cue 23	The ballooon drifts out of sight *Return to previous setting*	(Page 36)
Cue 24	Song 12 *Change to special "blue" lighting effect*	(Page 41)
Cue 25	End of Song 12 *Return to previous setting*	(Page 41)
Cue 26	As the balloon drifts out of sight *Fade to black-out*	(Page 47)

ACT II, SCENE 2

To open: Weird interior lighting

Cue 27	Song 14 *Special lighting and follow spots*	(Page 49)
Cue 28	End of Song 14 *Fade to black-out*	(Page 49)

ACT II, SCENE 3

To open: Sinister exterior lighting with reddish glow

Cue 29	**Halloweena**: "Ha! Ha! Ha!" *Flash of lightning. General lighting becomes even more sinister*	(Page 50)
Cue 30	**Halloweena**: "I command you — appear!" *Flash of lightning*	(Page 51)
Cue 31	The **Zombies** shuffle out *Return to opening sinister lighting*	(Page 52)
Cue 32	**Halloweena**: "Ha! Ha! Ha!" *Flash of lightning. General lighting becomes even more sinister*	(Page 54)

Cue 33   **Yeti** enters   (Page 54)
              The general lighting becomes brighter and less sinister

Cue 34   **Yeti** and **Cat**: "Abracadabra!!" There is a flash   (Page 55
              Black-out. Allow time for characters to change places,
              then bring up bright general lighting

Cue 35   **Woman** and **Girl**: "Farewell!" There is a flash   (Page 57)
              Black-out. Allow time for characters to exit, and then
                  return to previous setting

Cue 36   End of Song 16   (Page 58)
              Fade to black-out

ACT II, SCENE 4

To open: General exterior lighting

Cue 37   Song 17   (Page 61)
              House lights up (optional)

Cue 38   **Fit** and **Mabel** exit   (Page 61)
              House lights down and fade to black-out

Cue 39   **Town Crier** enters   (Page 61)
              Spotlight on **Town Crier**

Cue 40   **Town Crier** exits   (Page 62)
              Take out spotlight

ACT II, SCENE 5

To open: Bright general lighting. Follow spots

No cues

EFFECTS PLOT

ACT I

Cue 1   **Bessie**: "Are [local reference] having a sale?   (Page 10)
Loud crash inside town hall

Cue 2   End of Song 4   (Page 13)
Loud crash inside town hall

Cue 3   **Halloweena** makes a magic pass   (Page 18)
Flash

Cue 4   **Halloweena** makes magic pass   (Page 18)
Flash

Cue 5   **Town Crier**: "Make way for His Worship the   (Page 21)
    Mayor of Merrydale"
Fanfare

Cue 6   **Fit** and **Mabel**: "That one!"   (Page 24)
Clap of thunder

Cue 7   **Halloweena** makes a magic pass   (Page 26)
Flash

Cue 8   **Halloweena** raises her arms   (Page 26)
Flash

Cue 9   **Halloweena**: "Ha! Ha! Ha!"   (Page 35)
Violent storm effect. Claps of thunder, howling winds, etc.

ACT II

Cue 10   End of Song 11   (Page 36)
Violent storm effect. Claps of thunder, howling blizzard, etc.

Cue 11   The balloon drifts out of sight   (Page 36)
Storm subsides. Fade out sound effects

Cue 12   To open ACT II, Scene 3   (Page 49)
Ground mist

www.ingramcontent.com/pod-product-compliance
Lightning Source LLC
LaVergne TN
LVHW051757080426
835511LV00018B/3342